The Crafter's Book of Clever Ideas

Awesome Craft Techniques for Handmade Craft Projects

Andrea Currie

&

Cliff Currie

The Crafter's Book of Clever Ideas

Awesome Craft Techniques for Handmade Craft Projects

Andrea Currie

&

Cliff Currie

Cincinnati, Ohio

Table of Contents

Chapter 5

An Important Note for Our Readers

Let's face it. Crafting can sometimes be a full contact sport. For that reason, we recommend that you avoid any unwanted bumps, bruises, burns and headaches by following the manufacturer's directions on your supplies and by using applicable protective gear for yourself and your work surface. Always keep plenty of newspaper, heat resistant mats, eye protection, hand protection and painter's masks nearby and *never* let children craft unsupervised.

Introduction

Welcome to the wondrous world of *The Crafter's Book of Clever Ideas*. While you explore the pages of our colorful book, we are confident that you'll find fantastic handmade gift ideas, fun projects to share at your next craft party, unique ways to manipulate common and uncommon materials and a myriad of clever techniques that are sure to get your creative juices flowing. So grab your glue guns, glitter and hammers, and let's get this crafty adventure started!

Throughout the book, when you see the craft party icon, it means the project you're looking at is perfect for craft parties with friends. Have everyone gather their supplies and start crafting like crazy!

craft party!

1 The Kitsch Factor

Kill Them with Cuteness

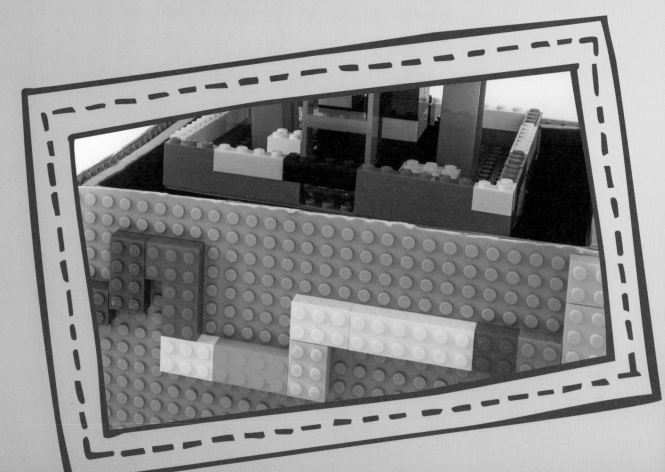

Tropical Vessels

Her Mini Pineapple Succulent

Who said plants couldn't have costumes? Turn a cute little succulent into an even cuter mini pineapple with an inexpensive glass jar and a little enamel paint!

TOOLS & MATERIALS

Tiny succulent

Tiny oblong glass candleholder

Yellow enamel paint

High quality brush

Brown or green medium-tip permanent marker

Fishnet stockings or netting

Small strip of jute (optional)

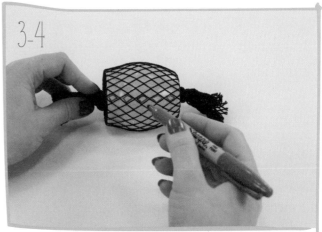

3. Slide the project into the fishnet stocking and knot both ends tightly.

4. Use the stocking as your guide for the diamond pattern around the entire piece. Draw the pattern between the diamond openings with a permanent marker

5. Remove the stocking, then bake the candleholder according to the instructions on the enamel paint bottle.

6. Plant the succulent and, if desired, wrap a jute bow around the top.

1. Clean the glass with rubbing alcohol before painting.

2. Paint the outside of your glass candleholder with two thin coats of yellow enamel paint, allowing the paint to dry between coats.

Designer Tip
Add neon and shimmer paint combinations for a wildly colorful pallet.

His Mini Palm Tree

It only takes a little brown enamel paint and a few fern sprigs to create a palm tree mirage on your windowsill or a fun palm tree grove for a luau party!

TOOLS & MATERIALS

Straight or tapered vase

Brown enamel paint

Real or fake foliage

1. Clean the glass with rubbing alcohol, then paint the vase with two coats of brown enamel paint, allowing the paint to dry between coats.

2. Bake the vase according to the instructions on the enamel paint bottle.

3. Add foliage and enjoy!

Felt Cactus Friends

Her Sweet Cactus Friend

Not only is this little cactus perfect for people who can't seem to keep plants alive, but it is also a great gift for people who need a secret hiding spot for stuff . . . you know, like chocolate!

TOOLS & MATERIALS

6" (15cm) white foam egg

4"-wide (10cm-wide) flower pot

2" × 4" (5cm × 10cm) saucers (one for the top and one for the bottom)

Chalkboard paint (optional)

Brown acrylic paint (optional)

Serrated knife for foam

Two 9" × 12" (23cm × 30cm) green felt sheets

Small 3" × 7$\frac{1}{2}$" (7.5cm × 19cm) strip of purple, pink or yellow felt (for flower)

Hot glue gun and hot glue

E6000 or a super glue

Sewing pins

Pinking shears

Designer Tip

Felt is quite stretchy, so make sure you have your felt stretched and formed enough on all sides before you glue it into place!

1. Paint one saucer brown and paint the lip of the flower pot with chalkboard paint (or leave them both plain if you prefer).

2. Cut the bottom 2" (5cm) off of the egg (this is your base).

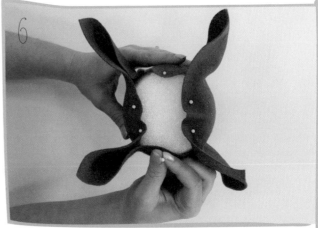

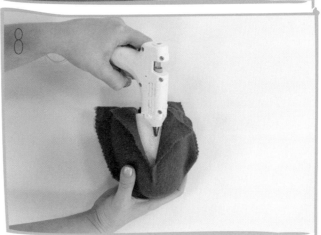

3. Round the peak of the egg by rolling it on a hard surface.

4. Take a 9" × 12" (23cm × 30cm) piece of felt and drape it over the egg.

5. Start forming the felt to the egg by pulling it down and stretching it toward the base.

6. Stretch and pin the four sides of the felt into the bottom of the base. This will create four evenly spaced wings of felt.

7. Pinch the wings together and use pinking shears to cut off the excess so you have about a ½" (1cm remaining on each wing.

8. Open each wing and add a generous line of hot glue to the foam from top to bottom. Quickly pinch the two felt pieces back together, smoothing as you pinch.

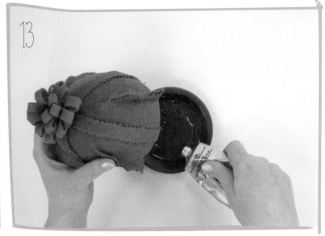

9. With pinking shears, cut two 1" (2.5cm) strips from your other felt sheet and glue them to your cactus, running from one side to the other. They will overlap at the top.

10. Cut a 3½"-wide × 7"-long (9cm × 18cm) strip of purple felt. Add a strip of hot glue to the bottom and fold.

11. On the fold, cut ½" (1cm) notches every 1" (2.5cm) or so.

12. Roll your felt flower up and place it onto the cactus with a dollop of hot glue.

13. Adhere your cactus to the brown saucer with a super-strong glue like E6000.

14. Wait for everything to dry, then fill the pot with goodies and place the cactus on top!

His Felt Venus Flytrap

Everyone loves a buddy with a dark side, which is why I couldn't resist making a felt version of the Venus flytrap! Not only will he protect your secret stash of thumb drives, but he'll also gladly hold your phone or other small devices in his mouth.

TOOLS & MATERIALS

One 9" × 12" (23cm × 30cm) medium green felt sheet

One 9" × 6" (23cm × 15cm) light green felt sheet

A scrap piece of red or pink felt (for the tongue)

6" (15cm) white foam egg

4" (10cm) wide flower pot

2" × 4" (5cm × 10cm) saucers (one for the top and bottom)

Hot glue gun and hot glue

Serrated knife for foam

E6000 or a super glue

Sewing pins

1. Follow steps 1–3 of Her Sweet Cactus Friend.

2. Cut a triangle mouth in the foam by cutting diagonally down. Leave at least 2" (5cm) between the mouth and the base of the egg.

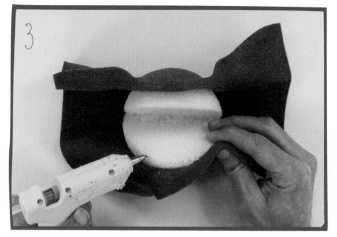

5. Add a strip of hot glue around the outside of the mouth and press down. Cut the excess felt away from the outer lips, but leave the excess felt around the base for the leaves.

6. Fold the light green felt into the mouth (like a taco), then add glue to the inside of the lips and press down.

7. Cut away the excess felt but leave a 1" (2.5cm) border for the teeth.

8. Cut triangles from the remaining light green felt to form the teeth.

9. Cut a tongue shape out of the pink or red felt and adhere it to the inside of the mouth.

10. Cut the excess felt on the sides into leaf shapes and, if needed, glue them into an upright position.

11. Follow steps 13–14 of Her Sweet Cactus Friend.

3. Place the base of the head in the middle of the medium green felt sheet.

4. Stretch the felt up and around the outside of the entire mouth. You should have two wings at the seams of the mouth.

Foodie Drink Charms

Her Cheese Wine Charms

These easy, cheesy polymer clay wine charms are a must-have for all wine lovers. Plus they're a perfect host or hostess gift set.

TOOLS & MATERIALS

2 oz. (5g) of white polymer clay

Parchment paper work surface

Aluminum foil-lined baking pan

Medium yellow, saffron yellow, bright-red and tan acrylic paint

Paint brushes

3" (75cm) head pins or flat pins (for jewelry making)

Pliers and a wire cutter

16-gauge wire

BBQ skewer

Clay knife

¹/₂" (1cm) wooden dowel or thick pen

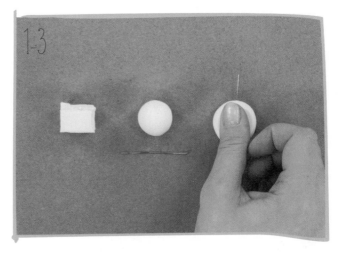

1. Roll six 1" (2.5cm) cubes of clay into balls.

2. Stick a flat pin directly through the center of each ball.

3. Set the balls on your work surface and squish down with your thumb.

Designer Tip
If a glossy look is desired, use a polymer clay glaze, which can be applied after baking.

21

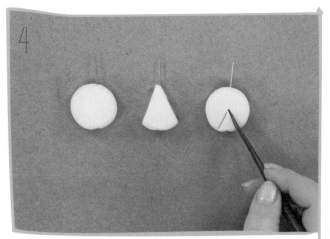

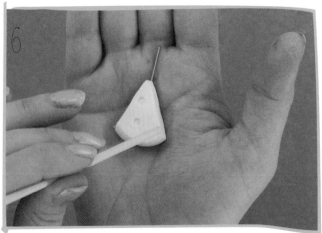

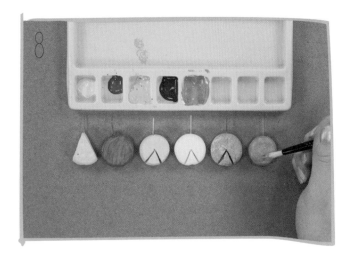

4. On three shapes, use the clay knife to score a triangle in the circle.

5. Leave two shapes uncut.

6. Create a slice of swiss cheese by cutting the two side edges off and adding dots with both ends of a BBQ skewer.

7. Place the piece on the aluminum foil-covered baking sheet and bake according to the instructions.

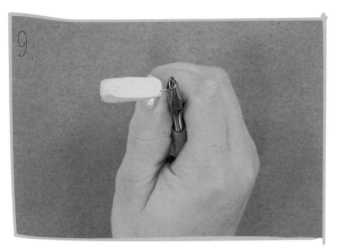

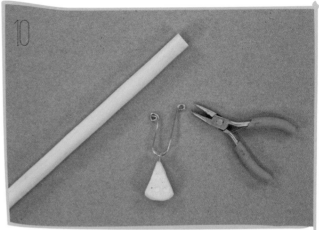

8. Once fully cooled, paint your pieces according to the picture.

Bright yellow = Swiss

Red = Gouda

Saffron = Cheddar

White = Brie

Yellow with dry brush brown = Fontina

Yellow with heavy tan brush = Dry Jack Cheese

9. Use your pliers to curl the end of the jewelry wire into a loop.

10. Cut a 3½" (9cm) long piece of 16-gauge copper wire and form it around a dowel to create a long U shape.

11. Slide the charm onto the wire and curl both sides of the wire to the outside of the U.

Designer Tip

Avoid unwanted specks in your clay projects by keeping your hands and work surface clean. Protect acrylic paints by lightly spraying them with an acrylic sealer or painting on a clear enamel finish.

His Pretzels for Your Beer

These polymer clay pretzel beer markers are great for dudes, dads or anyone who loves the old-time tradition of beer and pretzels! No party, especially one surrounding sports, should go without a bowl of faux pretzel beer markers. Just make sure everyone knows they're fake!

TOOLS & MATERIALS

2 oz. (5g) of medium brown polymer clay

Tiny bit of white polymer clay

Rubber bands

Various colored pony beads

Clay knife

Parchment paper work surface

Aluminum foil-lined baking pan

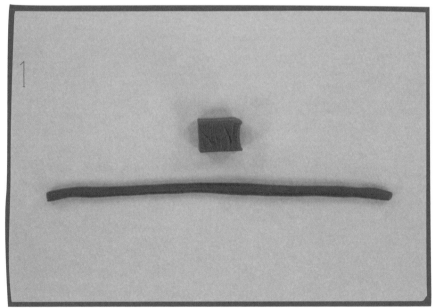

1. Use your hands to roll a 1" (2.5cm) cube of clay until it's 8" (20cm) long.

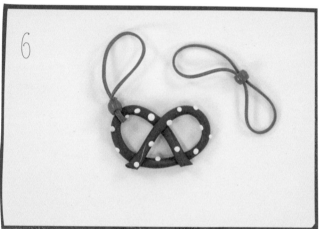

2. Hold both ends of the clay and wrap it into a loose bow shape. Press the clay where it crosses in the center and at the ends.

3. If needed, cut the excess from the ends.

4. Ball up tiny pieces of white clay and press them into the front of the pretzel.

5. Bake the clay according to the instructions on the clay package.

6. Once cooled, add a pony bead to a rubber band and slip knot it around the pretzel.

Fake Spills

craft party!

TOXIC WASTE

Her Button Spill Paperweight

Here we have the perfect gift for a crafty friend and a great project that puts all those loose buttons to work!

TOOLS & MATERIALS

Hot glue gun

4 long sticks of hot glue

Short glass container with flat sides (preferable)

About 7 large buttons

About 10 medium buttons

About 10 small buttons

About 5 tiny buttons

Craft tweezers

Fast-drying multi-surface super glue

Parchment paper or hot glue surface

4" × 4" (10cm × 10cm) piece of felt

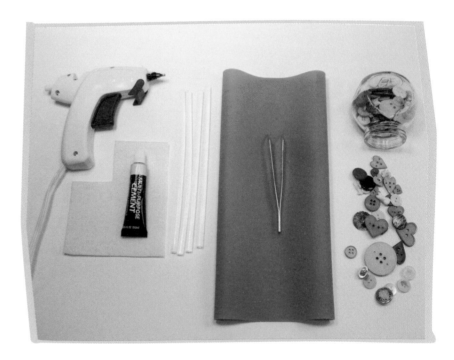

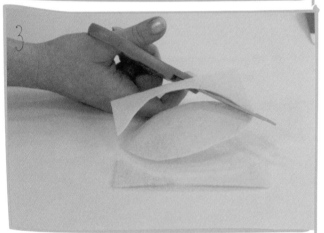

1. Put glue along the edges of the large buttons, then place them into the bottom of the tipped container with tweezers.

2. Add the medium and the small buttons next to and on top of the large buttons. When adding glue, place it along the area of the button that will touch the other buttons

3. Cut the felt into a spill shape by rounding the corners and adding swoops.

4. Add a very large dollop of hot glue to the edge of the felt piece and squish the edge of the container down into it.

5. Glue small, medium and large buttons along the felt. Make sure to overlap the edge of the felt.

6. Glue small, medium and large buttons to the middle.

7. Cover the gaps by gluing small and tiny buttons on top.

8. Use fast-drying glue to fill in all of the gaps with small and tiny buttons.

9. Allow the project to cool completely before you pick it up off the parchment paper.

His Toxic Spill Deterrent

Here's a fun hot glue craft inspired by one of my all time favorite TV shows, *The Simpsons*. Use it as a way to ward off people who like to snoop through the papers on your desk or as a funny way to mark those truly hazardous projects that you've been ignoring for the last few months.

TOOLS & MATERIALS

Small tin can (I used a small tomato paste can)

Rocks

4 long sticks of hot glue

Bright green enamel paint

Paintbrush

4" × 4" (10cm × 10cm) piece of felt

3" × 4" (7.5cm × 10cm) rectangle and a 2" (5cm) circle of white paper

1/2" (1cm) tall stencil letters

Red pen

Mod Podge

Foam brush

Heat gun

1. When you open your can, make sure to leave at least a ¹/₂" (1cm) of the lid attached to the can.

2. Wash and dry the can thoroughly.

3. Add rocks and glue just inside of the can lip, then push the lid back into place. This makes the can heavy enough to act as a paperweight.

4. Cut a spill-like shape out of your felt.

5. Add a large dollop of glue at the edge of the felt and place the mouth of the can over it.

6. Work your hot glue from the mouth of the can to the end of the felt. Make sure it goes slightly over the edges of the felt on all sides.

7. If your "spill" is a bit wrinkled, and you prefer a smoother look, hit it with a heat gun!

8. Once the glue is completely dry, cover the glue with two coats of bright green enamel paint using a higher quality acrylic brush.

9. Stencil "Toxic Spill" onto a 3" × 4" (7.5cm × 10cm) piece of white paper. For the top of the can, cut out a 2" (5cm) white paper circle and draw red triangles on it in a toxic symbol formation. Use Mod Podge to adhere both pieces to the can with a foam brush.

10. Allow everything to dry and then enjoy!

Designer Tip

Have some ice water on standby to cool pesky burns. Use a wooden, heat-resistant cutting board under your nonstick paper. For an even firmer surface, use a meltable resin.

Fountains of Youth

TOOLS & MATERIALS

Fake trumpet-shaped flowers

A few sprigs of smaller flowers

Fake grass

Small garden statue (snail, bird)

Small but deep decorative bowl

50 ft. (15m) of garden wire (you won't need all of it)

18" (46cm) garden hook

A plastic colander (strainer) that fits inside the bowl and is the same height as the bowl

An indoor fountain pump kit with tubing (found online or at pool stores)

Heavy-duty scissors

Water-resistant glue or hot glue

Small whiffle ball, approximately 1" (2.5cm) in diameter

Her Whimsical Garden Fountain

Bring the outdoors in with this adorable garden-themed fountain!

1. Make sure your tubing reaches from the bottom of the bowl to about 9" (23cm) above the rim of the bowl.

2. Make a candy cane shape by wrapping garden wire tightly around the tube and securing the end of the wire to the upper half of the wrapped tube.

3. Cut the fake grass to the size of the bowl's opening.

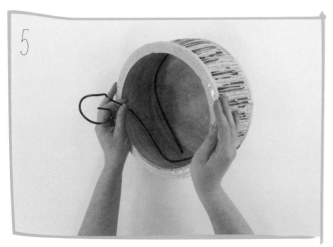

4. Cut or drill a hole in the left-hand side of the colander. If needed, cut a hole at the bottom of the colander to allow the power cord to exit.

5. Wrap the garden hook around the inside of the bowl, leaving the top of the hook 5" (13cm) above the top of the bowl rim.

6. Feed the wrapped tube through the left side of the grass and through the left side of the colander. Insert the end of the tube into the top of the water pump. Insert the structure into the bowl.

7. Wrap the tube around the garden hook.

8. Cut a small hole in the whiffle ball and insert it onto the end of the tube with water-resistant glue or hot glue.

9. Cut one large trumpet-shaped flower open and glue it around the end of the tube.

10. Hide the water tube by wrapping and adhering more large trumpet flowers, smaller flowers and other floral embellishments around the structure.

11. Adhere wire to the base of the small statue with water-resistant super glue and tie it onto the grass.

12. Fill the bowl with water and turn on the pump. Adjust the water flow accordingly.

His Building Block Fountain

Build a fun and interactive fountain with your favorite building blocks. I used Lego pieces because *I love Lego*!

TOOLS & MATERIALS

Lots of building blocks (Lego)

Building block sheets

Quick-dry, water-resistant glue

Fountain pump kit with tubing

Plastic colander the size and height of the bowl

Square bowl

Heavy-duty scissors

Power drill

1. Create at least two different tiers by cutting the block sheets to the desired size. Leave the base sheet 1" (2.5cm) smaller than the circumference of the bowl.

2. Drill a hole the size of your tubing into each sheet and the center top of the colander.

3. Build the desired columns onto each sheet around the drilled holes.

4. Use quick-dry, water-resistant glue to adhere the tiers together.

5. Adhere the structure to the top of the colander with quick-dry glue, making sure the holes align.

Designer Tip

Find small fountain pump kits online or in a pool supply store. Make sure your pump has enough room between the bottom of the bowl and the pump. Add water every week or as it evaporates, and clean monthly with a light cleanser.

6. Cut the block sheets to the size of the outside of the bowl and adhere with quick-dry glue.

7. Attach the tube to the water pump base and feed the tube through the structure.

8. Place the pump inside the container, fill with water and start the pump! Adjust the water pressure accordingly.

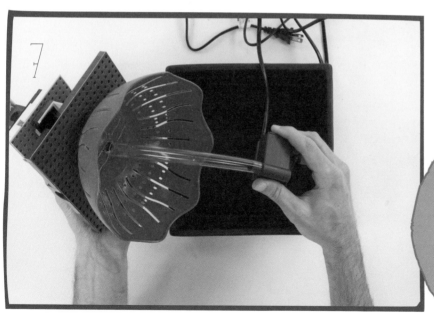

Designer Tip

Although it looks like a toy, we must stress that fountains should only be handled when unplugged and with adult supervision. Make sure your hands are not wet when plugging the pump back into the wall. Never run the pump when the water is low, and make sure the water is clear of any debris.

2 Fun & Functional

Handmade Accents for Home & Work

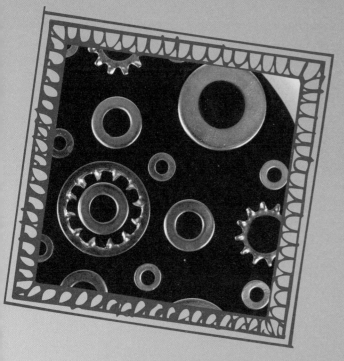

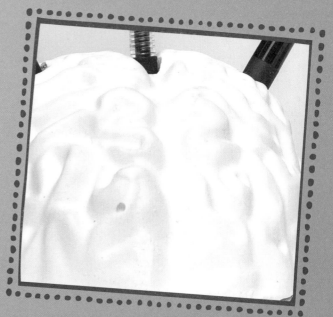

Crush on
Crushed Glass

His Geode Bookends

Hold your favorite books together with some heavy-duty geodes! It's amazing how a few simple materials can create such a neat effect!

TOOLS & MATERIALS

5" (12.5cm) square bricks

Hammer

Gloves

Protective goggles

Super glue like E6000

Felt

Silver tumbled crushed glass (usually found in the party decorating section)

Dark silver or black fine-grit glitter

Popsicle stick

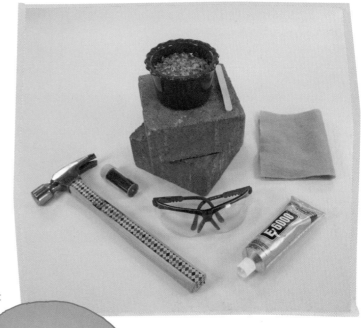

Designer Tip

Kid-friendly alternatives to glass include sequins, small fish tank pebbles or chunky glitter.

1. In an outdoor space, round off the corner of your bricks with a hammer.

2. Also hammer out a small divot in the center of each brick. This doesn't have to be perfect!

3. Wipe off the excess dust with a damp rag.

4. Spread glue in the divots with the popsicle stick.

Designer Tip

For even more protection, cover the brick with a towel and always wear eye and hand protection. Keep hands clean of super glue by wearing latex gloves.

5. Add crushed glass.

6. Gently shake off the excess crushed glass and sprinkle on the black glitter.

7. Glue the felt pieces to the bottom and side of each brick.

Designer Tip

Try spray painting over the crushed glass with metallic silver or gold paint. Or use different colored crushed glass and glitter for a sparkly contrast!

Her Crushed Glass Candleholder

Create a super chic and shimmery candleholder for pennies on the dollar by using tumbled crushed glass and thrift store votive candleholders.

TOOLS & MATERIALS

Votive candleholder

E6000 or other super glue

Craft stick

Tumbled crushed glass (the lightest color you can find)

Glitter

Latex gloves

Felt

Parchment paper

Fake candle

Designer Tip

Although crushed glass is tumbled, it still can be a little sharp. Always handle with care and protect surfaces that projects will be resting on.

1. In 3" (7.5cm) increments, use a craft stick to spread a thin layer of E6000 across the outside of the glass.

2. Quickly add some crushed glass and repeat until the candleholder is covered.

3. Add glitter.

4. Set the candleholder on top of the parchment paper in a well ventilated area.

5. Once fully dry, you may need to fill in a few gaps with more crushed glass.

6. Add a felt circle to the bottom of the glass.

Clay Coasters
that Sparkle

Her Stenciled Glitter Coaster

OMG (Oh My Glitter), this project is so much fun! I can't wait to have a glitter clay coaster party! Create your own truly unique coaster by mixing and matching clay colors, glitter colors and stencil shapes.

TOOLS & MATERIALS

4¼" (11cm) round clay cutter

Clay in your colors of choice (1 oz. [30g] = one 4¼" [11cm] round coaster)

Glitter in your colors of choice

Plastic stencils in various designs

Foil

Baking Sheet

Oven

Felt

Hot glue gun and hot glue or E6000 super glue

Clay roller or clay pasta machine

Designer Tip

Polymer clay is highly addictive, but make sure you are using tools meant only for polymer clay, and always use an oven in a well ventilated room.

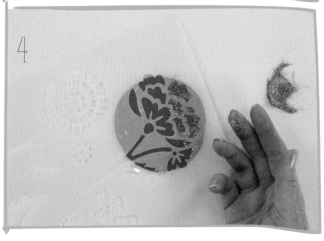

1. Roll clay out to about .089" (2.269mm). This is a #9 on most clay pasta machines.

2. Cut a 4¼" (11cm) circle.

3. Apply the stencil design to the desired area of the coaster and rub it into the clay so it is essentially sticking to the clay.

4. Dab your finger into a pile of glitter and rub it firmly onto the clay. Using your finger to apply the glitter is not only fun, but it also gives you control and the option to blend in different colors of glitter.

5. Brush off the excess glitter before gently removing the stencil.

6. Place the coaster on the foil-lined baking sheet and bake according to the clay instructions.

7. After baking, you can scratch any unwanted loose glitter off with your fingernail. The stenciled glitter will stay permanently!

8. Trace a felt circle and adhere it to the bottom of the coaster with hot glue or super glue.

9. Repeat these steps for the rest of your coasters.

His Man Cave Coasters

These coasters are great for all of the gearheads and rock star man caves.

TOOLS & MATERIALS

4¼" (11cm) round clay cutter

4 oz. (113g) or 2 packages of black polymer clay

Clay roller or clay pasta machine

Black felt for bottom

Various sized washers and plumbers washers (the spikey kind)

Parchment paper (for work surface)

Baking pan

Oven

Hot glue gun and hot glue or E6000

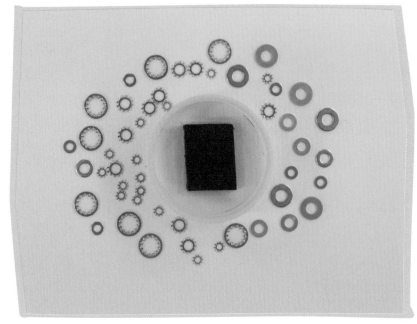

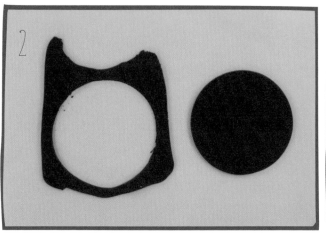

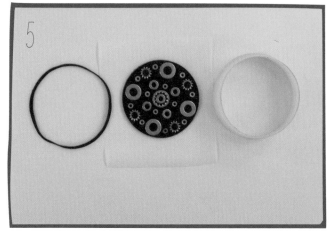

4. Once you are happy with your design, firmly press each washer into the clay so it's flush with the clay.

5. The pressing will make the edges sloppy, so use your circle cutter to create a clean circle once more.

6. Place the parchment paper onto the baking sheet and bake the coasters according to the clay instructions.

8. Once baked, trace a felt circle and adhere it to the bottom of the coaster with hot glue or super glue.

9. Repeat these steps for the rest of your coasters.

1. Roll the clay out to about .089" (2.269mm). This is a #9 on most clay pasta machines.

2. Cut a 4¼" (11cm) circle and remove the excess clay.

3. Gently lay out your design and keep each washer ¼" (6mm) away from the edges and each other. Don't press them in yet!

Designer Tip
If you have a hard time getting washers flush with the coaster, use a craft stick or craft tweezers to embed them.

By the Sea Apothecary Toppers

His Glow-in-the-Dark Sea Urchin

There are two reasons to make a glow-in-the-dark polymer clay sea urchin: 1.) Sea urchins are hard to find intact. 2.) Glowing sea urchins don't exist. If that isn't enough to excite you, then you must not be human.

TOOLS & MATERIALS

1 oz. (30g) glow-in-the-dark polymer clay

Ball chain necklace

Small apothecary jar

Ball end tool

Poker tool

E6000 or other super glue

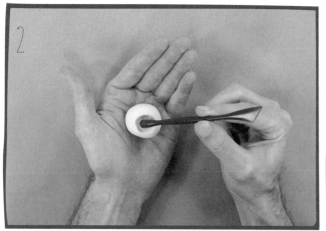

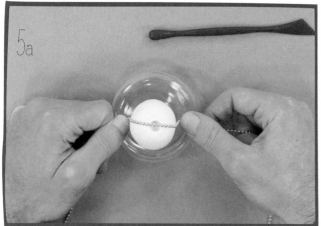

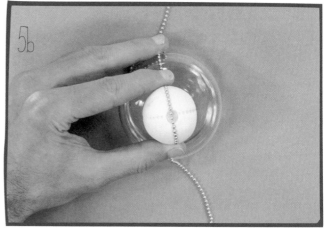

1. Roll the clay into a ball.

2. Hollow out the ball with the ball end tool.

3. Place the clay on top of the apothecary jar knob.

4. Press a hole with the large poker tool into the top.

5. Stretch the ball chain tight and imprint it into the clay in at least four different directions.

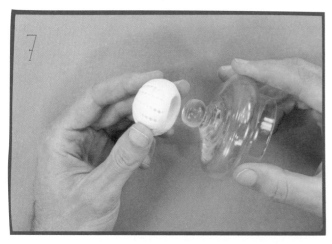

6. Gently remove the clay from the apothecary jar and bake it according to the clay instructions.

7. While still warm from baking, place the knob back onto the jar with a dollop of super glue.

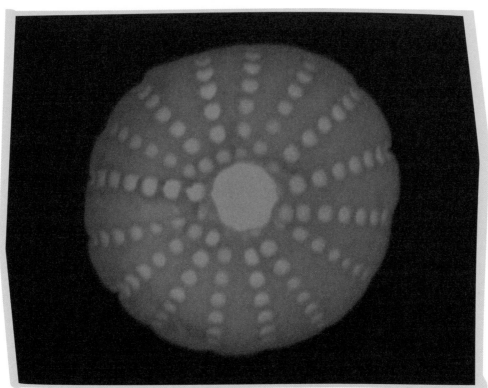

Your glow-in-the-dark sea urchin with the lights off.

Her Glowing Barnacles

Just like Cliff's project, these glowing barnacles are one of a kind and simple to create. However, my project is the only one that will have people shouting, "Great glowing barnacles, Batman!" and, therefore, I win.

TOOLS & MATERIALS

2 oz. (55g) or 1 package glow-in-the-dark polymer clay

Small apothecary jar

Ball end tool

Poker tool

Flat craft knife tool

Bakeable adhesive for polymer clay

E6000 or other super glue

Designer Tip

Make a tinfoil tent to protect your lighter colored clay projects from burning or from residual food-spill smoke in your oven

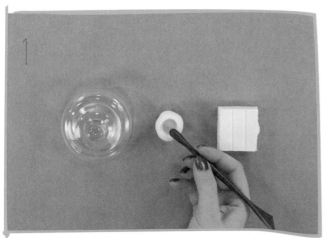

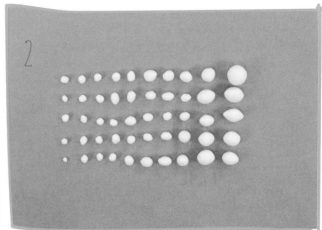

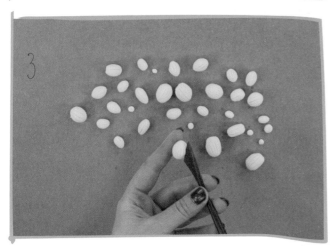

1. Using ½ oz. (15g) of the clay (one stick), follow steps 1–3 of His Glow-in-the-Dark Sea Urchin.

2. Roll the remaining 1½ oz.(40g) of clay into small, medium and large oblong balls.

3. Add stripes to each ball with the flat craft knife.

4. Place a dollop of bakeable adhesive onto the clay, and use the ball end tool to press a barnacle into it. Do this for each barnacle, holding them gently as you add more.

5. With a thick, pointy tool, add a hole in each barnacle.

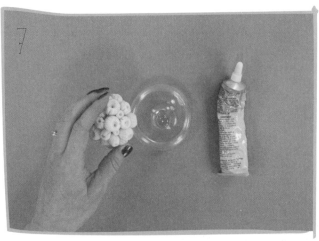

6. Gently remove the entire piece from the apothecary jar and bake it according to the clay instructions.

7. While still warm from baking, place the topper back onto the jar with a dollop of super glue.

Your completed barcacle topper.

Designer Tip

Use bakeable polymer clay adhesive when you need to attach smaller clay pieces together. The home decor possibilities are endless with these sea creature bobbles. Freshen up a cabinet or even a plain candlestick.

Miniature Taxidermy Bulletin Boards

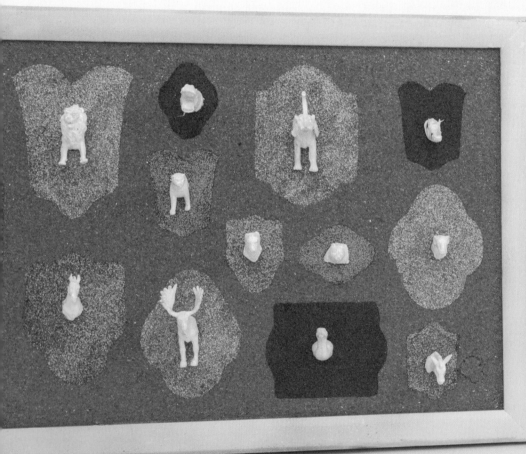
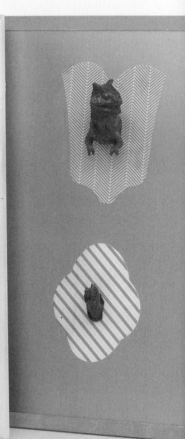

His Magnetic Dino Board

Protect your most important notes with your very own prehistoric bulletin board. Perfect for kids and geeks alike.

TOOLS & MATERIALS

Magnetic board

Small- and medium-sized dinosaurs

Small super-magnetic magnets

Heavy-duty scissors or saw

Various colors of enamel paint

Small paintbrushes

Various patterned papers

Mod Podge

E6000 or other super glue

Parchment paper

Template on page 184

Printer

Painters tape

1. Tape off the inside of the board and paint the frame with two coats of enamel paint.

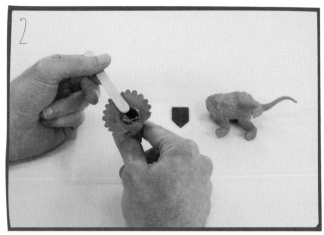

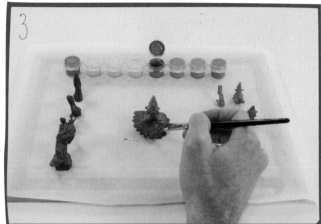

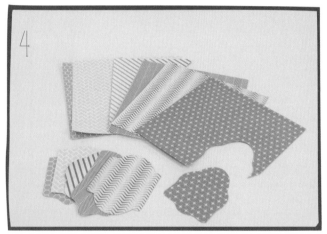

2. Cut the heads off of the dinosaurs and super glue them to the magnets (cut the magnets to size if needed). Rest them on parchment paper to dry.

3. Transfer the dino magnets to a parchment paper-covered magnetic board. Paint your dinosaurs with two coats of enamel paint.

4. Scan, print and cut out the taxidermy backers from the template, then trace the taxidermy backers onto the patterned paper. Cut out the paper backers and set them aside.

5. Brush Mod Podge onto the back of the backer paper and place them on the magnetic board.

TOOLS & MATERIALS

Corkboard (preferably with an unfinished frame)

Small- and medium-sized animals

Flat-backed push-pins

Heavy-duty scissors or saw

White enamel paint

Small paintbrushes

Contact paper

Mod Podge

E6000 or other super glue

Parchment paper

Template on page 184

Printer

Various colored glitter

Permanent marker

Scrap foam or cardboard [at least 10" (25.4cm) tall and wide]

Craft knife

Self-healing mat

Her Glittered Taxidermy Corkboard

Add a little sparkle and whimsy to your workspace with a taxidermy board that screams animal bling.

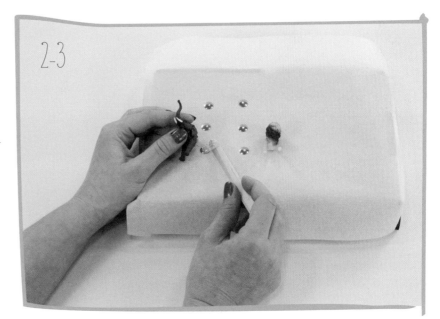

2-3

For the animals

1. Cut the heads off of the animals using heavy-duty scissors. Leave the front legs on some of the smaller animals.

2. Cover the scrap foam or cardboard in parchment paper and push your pins in.

3. Add a dollop of super glue to the tops of each pin and add the animal heads.

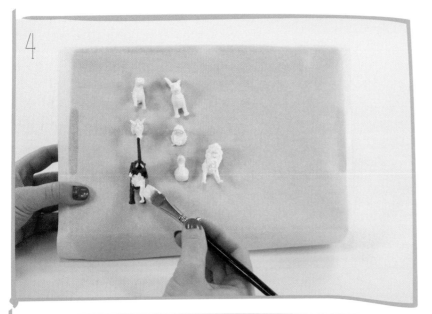

4. Add two coats of enamel paint, allowing the paint to dry between coats.

For the board

While you wait for the paint to dry, follow the steps below:

5. Scan, print and cut out the taxidermy backers from the template, one at 100% scale and one at 60% scale.

6. Cut the contact paper to the inside dimensions of the cork board.

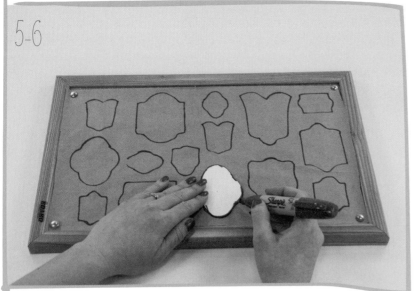

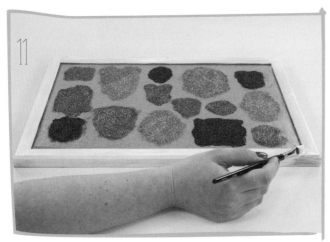

7. With a permanent marker, trace the taxidermy backers onto the contact paper in your desired layout.

8. Cut out the template with a craft knife.

9. Peel away the contact paper backer and place the sticky side onto the corkboard.

10. Brush a thin layer of Mod Podge over each taxidermy backer opening. Add glitter as you go.

11. Tap off any excess glitter, but before you peel back your contact paper, make sure to paint the frame of the corkboard.

12. Remove the contact paper and pin your animals into place.

Brain and Bedazzled Bud Vases

His Porcelain Pen Head

I've created a new style, and I call it zombie chic. I predict this brain organizer will become a must-have, after the apocalypse, for all of the hard-working zombies. Better make yours soon, because you will not want to be left behind when we all start obsessing over "braaaaains!"

TOOLS & MATERIALS

Plastic brain mold used for Jell-o (I found mine on Amazon)

Plaster of paris

Disposable bowl/bucket and wood stirrer

Large and small drill bit and drill

Felt

Quick-dry glue

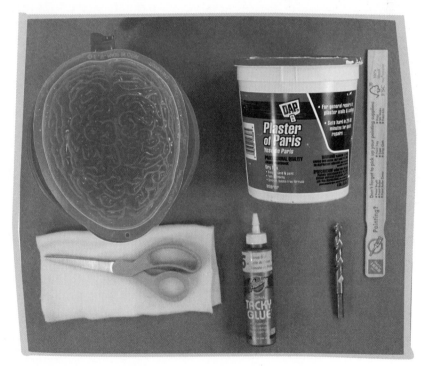

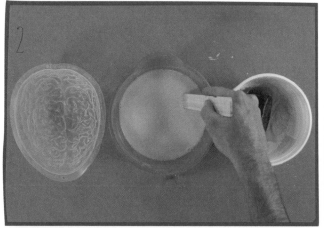

1. Fill your mold with water and dump it into your mixing bowl.

2. Stir in cups of plaster of paris until you get a consistency that is thicker than milk but not as thick as yogurt.

3. Pour the plaster into the mold and set it aside in a safe place. Put braces underneath the mold if it feels like it's going to tip over.

4. Once the plaster is completely dry, pop it out of the mold. If it doesn't pop out, use a small drill bit and drill a small hole through the mold at the top of the brain. When you reuse the mold, just cover the hole with a piece of tape.

5. To maintain the structural rigidity, drill no more than five holes into the brain using a large drill bit at a slow speed. You will need to clean the drill bit in between holes. These holes with hold your pens or other items

6. Cut the felt to size and glue it on with quick-dry glue.

Her Bedazzling Bud Vase

I prefer to think that, if I become a zombie, I'll still be attracted to all that sparkles. So I decided to spruce up all the bland little corners in my office with these simple, topsy-turvey and shimmery bud vases!

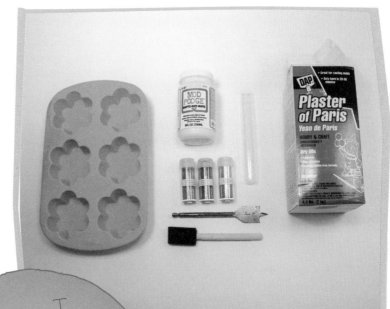

TOOLS & MATERIALS

Mixing bucket

Plaster of paris

Silicon flower molds

Test tubes

Glitter

Mod Podge

Foam Brush

1" (2.5cm) high container or lid

Popsicle stick

Drill with a ⁵/₈" (1.5cm) spade bit

Designer Tip

The box says 1 part water and 2 parts plaster of paris, but we've found you need more water, which is why we gauge the water by the volume of the mould. This may yield more mixture than expected, but that's better than not enough! Just have a few small molds hanging around in case you're caught with extra mixture.

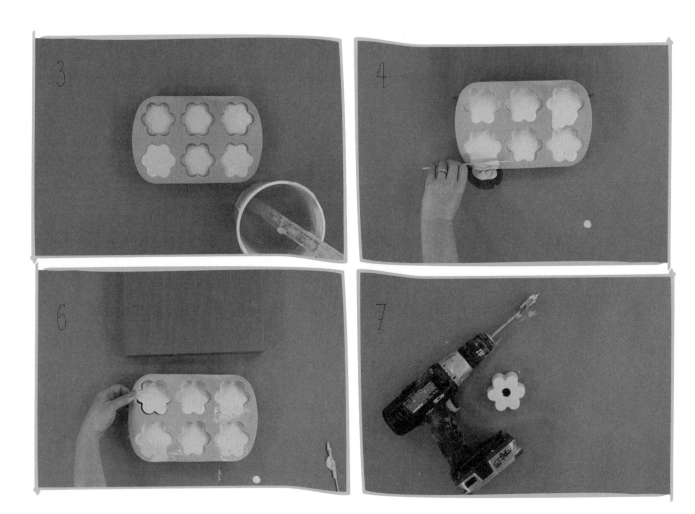

1. Fill the mold with water and pour it into the mixing bucket.

2. Mix plaster of paris into the water until you get a thicker-than-milk consistency.

3. Pour the mixture into the molds.

4. Tip the entire mold at an angle and place 1" (2.5cm) lid underneath. The plaster will run down at this angle, but don't worry!

5. Scrape off the excess plaster with a popsicle stick.

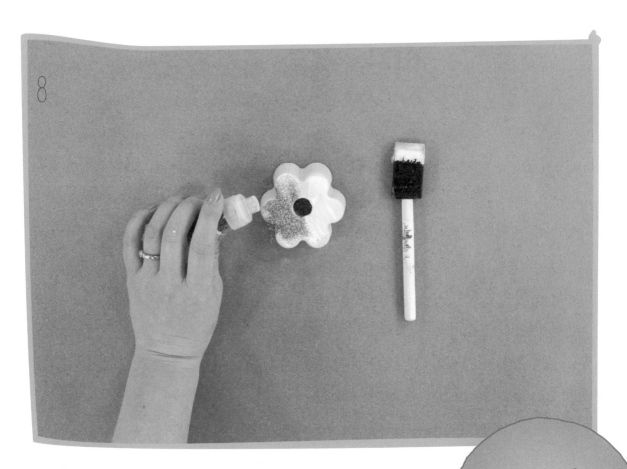

6. Once the plaster dry, pop it out of the mold.

7. Drill holes straight down into the center of the flower using a ⅝" (1.5cm) spade bit.

8. Cover in Mod Podge and your favorite color glitter! Place the test tubes into the holes, and you're ready to display a few flowers.

Designer Tip

For extra-strength glitter adhesion, hit your projects with clear acrylic sealer spray.

3 Let's Hang

Art & Other Neat Things

Wild Doggie Doo Bag Dispensers

TOOLS & MATERIALS

Small plastic sugar container large enough to fit a roll of doggie doo bags

Black, silver and gold Sharpie paint pens

6" (15cm) of ball chain with clasp (you can also use a thick rubber band)

Pliers

Designer Tip

Find small plastic condiment containers at value or dollar stores.

Her Leopard Print Doggie Doo Bag Dispenser

Hang one of these inexpensive sugar containers turned stylish doggie doo bag dispensers from your best friend's leash and avoid dog park embarrassment!

1. Pop off the twist lid with the pliers. This should reveal a hole that is perfect for the fastener.

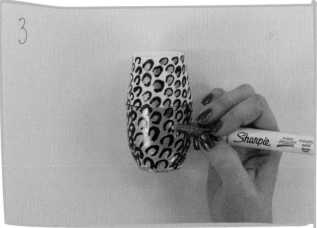

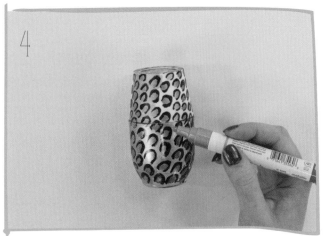

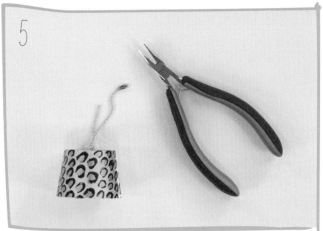

2. Make sure the lid is tightly closed and use the black Sharpie paint pen to draw angled half circles around the entire container. Don't worry about making them perfect.

3. Fill in the circles with the gold Sharpie paint pen.

4. Fill in the area between the pattern spots with the silver paint pen.

5. Run a ball chain through the center circle and clasp closed.

TOOLS & MATERIALS

Small plastic sugar container large enough to fit a roll of doggie doo bags

Black and white Sharpie paint pens.

6" (15cm) of ball chain with clasp

Pliers

6 rubber bands

His Tribal-Striped Doggie Doo Bag Dispenser

For a more masculine tribal doggie doo bag dispenser, simply add some hand-drawn stripes using rubber bands as your guide.

1. Pop off the twist lid with the pliers. This should reveal a hole that is perfect for the fastener.

2. Evenly space the six rubber bands lengthwise.

3. On the lower part, draw white upside-down V's using the rubber bands as your guide.

4. On the upper part draw black upside-down V's.

5. Remove the rubber bands and draw black lines where the rubber bands used to be.

6. Run a ball chain through the center circle and clasp closed.

Fishnet String Art

His Music Wavelength Art

I know what you are thinking. Fishnets have but one place in this world: 80's rock star bachelor parties. Well, unfortunately, you're wrong. The Currie household uses fishnet stockings for one reason and one reason only—crafting! So grab your neon fishnets and let's get this party started!

TOOLS & MATERIALS

Black poster board

Craft knife

Cutting board

Metal ruler

20" (51cm) of electric green fishnet stockings (about one leg)

About twenty 1" (2.5cm) pins

Hot glue gun and hot glue

Black Sharpie marker

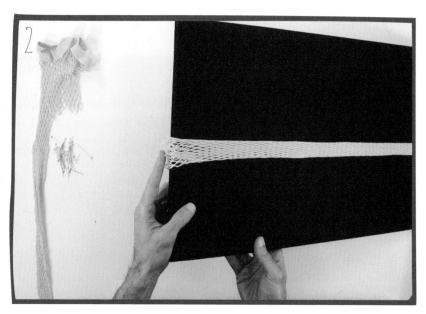

1. Use your metal ruler and craft knife to cut two pieces of 24" × 12" (61cm × 30.5cm) black poster board.

2. Cut a 20" (51cm) strip of fishnet off one leg of the stockings.

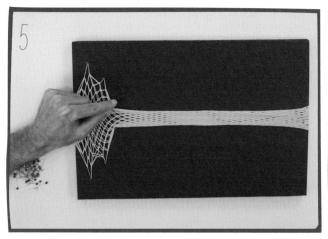

3. Loosely stretch the material across the front of your first piece of poster board, flip the board over and rest the excess fishnets on the back.

4. Add a border of hot glue around the entire board, including over the tails of the fishnet. Quickly press your second poster board on top of the back of your first one before the hot glue dries.

5. Using a tiny ball of hot glue on the end of each pin, make peaks and valleys.

6. Create peaks by pulling the fishnet an equal distance away from the middle.

7. Make valleys by pushing the fishnet toward the middle.

8. Once the desired shape is achieved, color the pinheads black with a permanent marker.

Her Fishnet Dreamcatcher

This dreamcatcher is great for the young and young at heart. Create your own majestic, no-fuss dreamcatcher with fishnet stockings, charms, feathers and beads.

TOOLS & MATERIALS

14-gauge wire (found at the hardware store)

Perler or Pony beads

8" (20.5cm) of fishnet stockings

Feathers

Sequins

String

Quick-dry glue

Wire cutters

Pliers

Fishing wire or decorative string

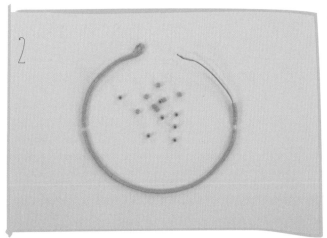

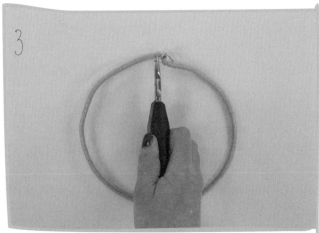

1. Cut an 18" (45.5cm) piece of 14-gauge wire, bend it into a circle (if it is not already bent) and use the pliers to twist one end shut.

2. Add the Perler or Pony beads.

3. Use your pliers to close the circle by twisting the open end into the closed end of the circle.

4. Secure the top middle of the fishnet to your closure loop.

5. Stretch the fishnet around the hoop, keeping the beads in the middle of the stocking. Make sure the stocking is on both sides of the beaded hoop.

6. Wrap one end of the fishnet to the top of the circle and stretch the fishnet all the way around, securing it at the starting point with a knot.

7. Hide the stretched fishnet by pushing it into the spaces between the beads.

8. Tie strings to the bottom of the hoop and attach the feathers.

9. Decorate with quick-drying glue and sequins.

10. Hang with fishing wire or decorative string.

Solar-Powered Cell Phone Hangers

His Chalkboard Solar Phone Charger

Decorate your space with functional art that uses a little bit of design wizardry to provide a safe place for mobile devices and, most important, charges said devices using the sun!

TOOLS & MATERIALS

Acrylic sign holder with hole for suction cup

Super-strong suction cups (we used FrogsFeet)

Decorative fabric

Precision scissors

Small solar panel with charging wire (found online)

Medium-sized drill bit and drill

Mod Podge

Industrial Velcro

Painter's tape

Medium-grit sandpaper

Chalkboard paint

Paintbrush

Foam brush

1. Sand the front side of the sign holder.

Designer Tip
You can find FrogsFeet suction cups and small solar panels with charging cables on Amazon.

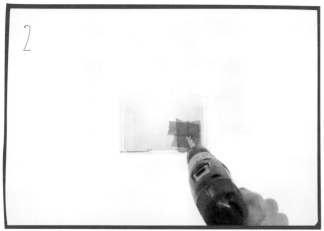

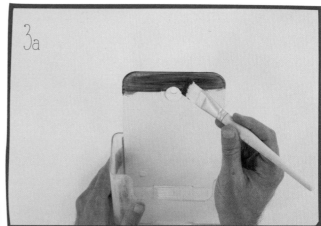

2. Drill a hole into the bottom of the back side of the sign holder. Use painter's tape to prevent the acrylic from cracking.

3. Using horizontal strokes, apply the first coat of blackboard paint to the entire sign hanger, except at the front and sides, which will be covered later.

4. Once dry, apply a second coat of blackboard paint using vertical strokes.

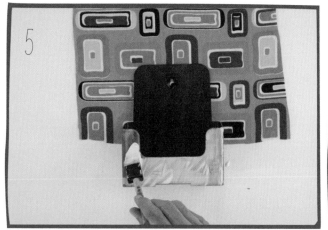

5. Apply Mod Podge to the front of the sign holder.

6. Place the sign holder onto the fabric and pull the sides of the fabric up.

7. Cut away the excess fabric using precision scissors.

8. Seal the fabric with a layer of Mod Podge.

9. Attach the Velcro to the back of the sign holder and the back of the solar panel.

10. Feed the charging wire through the lower hole.

11. Use Mod Podge to add a fabric decoration over the suction cup hole.

12. Hang and enjoy!

Her Swanky Phone Hanger

This swanky phone hanger blends an old craft tool (an embroidery hoop) and some fabulous retro vintage fabric with the technology of solar charging! This is the type of project that I like to call "craft to the future."

TOOLS & MATERIALS

Large oval embroidery hoop

Super-strong suction cups

Decorative fabric

Solid fabric (I used an old napkin so I didn't have to sew a hem)

Sewing machine and thread (if you need to sew a hem)

Ribbon

Buttons

Scissors

Small solar panel with charging wire

Hot glue and hot glue gun

String

Small screw hook

Acrylic paint

Brush

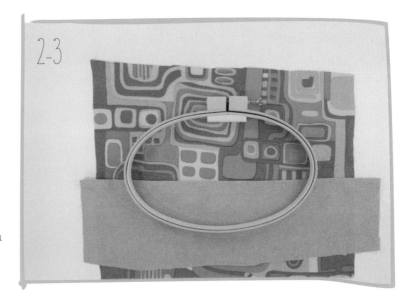

1. Paint the outside ring of the embroidery hoop whatever color you desire.

2. Cut the patterned fabric at least 3" (7.5cm) wider and longer than the embroidery hoop.

3. Cut the solid fabric to fit in the lower third of the embroidery hoop and, if needed, hem the top.

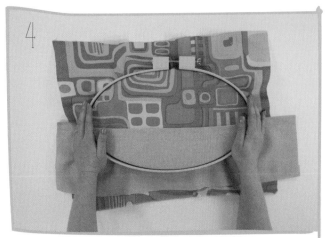

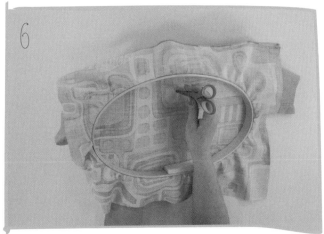

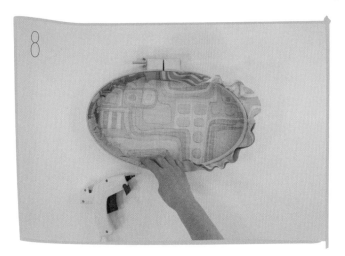

4. Place the fabric on top of the inner embroidery hoop and push the outer hoop over it.

5. Tighten the outer hoop.

6. Flip the hoop over and poke a hole in the lower portion of the patterned fabric *only*.

7. Cut the excess fabric to 1½" (3.8cm) outside of the hoop.

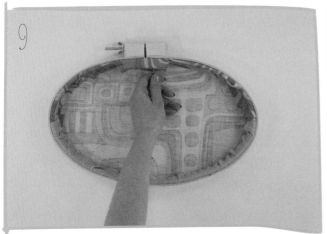

8. Fold the excess fabric into the hoop, securing it to the inside of the inner hoop with hot glue.

9. Screw the loop into the top of the embroidery hoop.

10. Hang the solar panel with string.

11. Decorate with ribbon and buttons

Designer Tip

For a completely no-sew project, use an old linen napkin as your front pouch piece. Or make a no-sew hem with an iron-on fusible webbing.

Breakfast Keychains

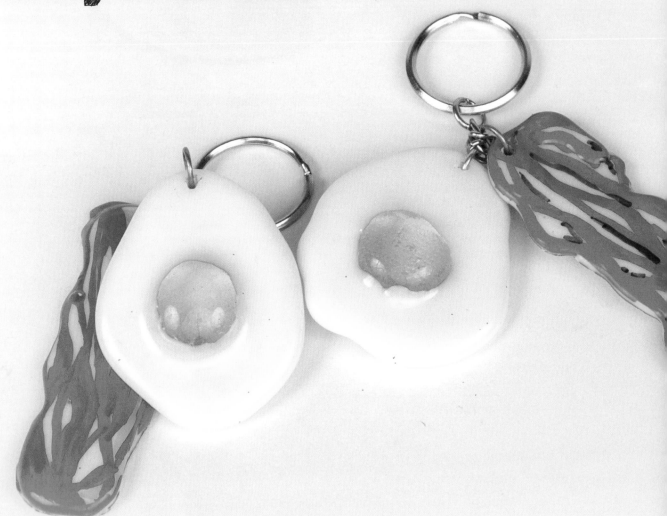

96

Her Resin Eggs

If you haven't already noticed, we like to melt things, so it's no surprise that we've added Mod Melts, a meltable resin, to our must-have list. You can easily melt this resin into Mod Melt molds or freehand it onto a heat-resistant surface. Naturally we did the latter and made breakfast keychains!

TOOLS & MATERIALS

White Mod Melt resin stick

Glass pebble

Yellow paper

Scissors or $1/2$" (1.3cm) circle punch

Mod Podge

Foam brush

High-heat hot glue gun (preferably with a precision tip)

Small drill bit and drill

Keychain hardware with jump ring

Heat-resistant surface such as hot glue gun helpers mat

Pliers

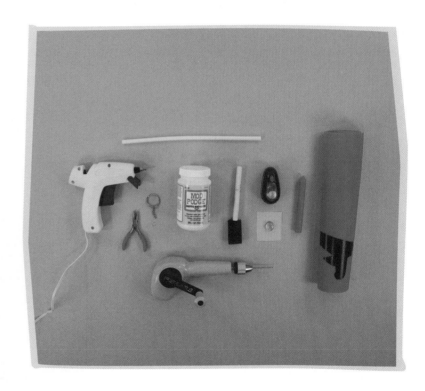

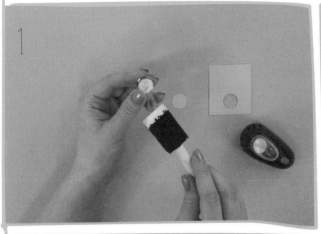

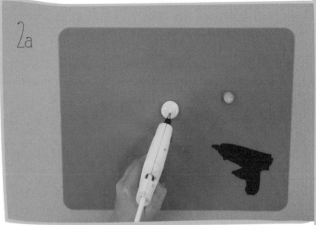

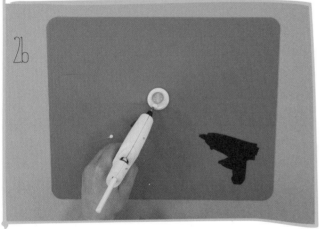

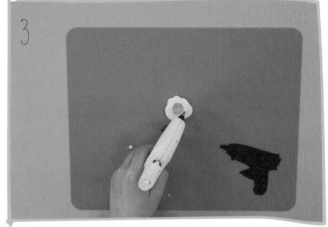

1. Cut out a piece of yellow paper and adhere it to the flat side of the pebble (this make the yolk). Wait until it's completely dry before moving onto the next step.

2. Create a mound of white Mod Melt resin (about the size of a quarter) and quickly drop your yolk in the center.

3. Continue adding white Mod Melt around the edges of the yolk.

4. By this time you should have a nice egg shape that is at least ¼" (6mm) deep.

5. Wait for it to cool (about 5 minutes).

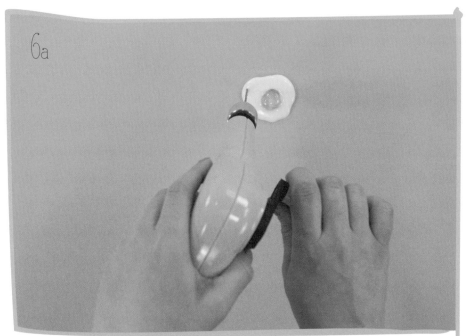

6. Drill a hole toward the top. Add a jump ring and secure it onto the keychain with pliers.

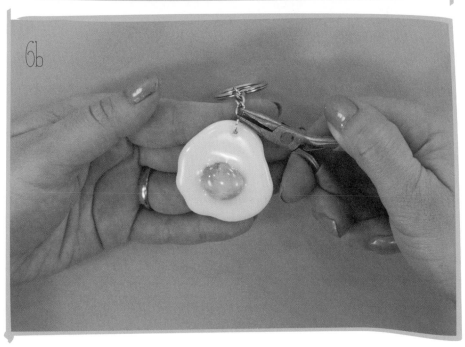

TOOLS & MATERIALS

White Mod Melt resin stick

Red oil-based Sharpie marker

Brown regular Sharpie marker

High-heat hot glue gun (preferably with a precision tip)

Small drill bit and drill

Keychain hardware with jump ring

Heat-resistant surface such as a hot glue gun helpers mat or parchment paper on a heat-resistant surface (I used the latter)

Pliers

Ruler

His Resin Bacon

You can't have eggs without bacon! Luckily Mod Melts makes it easier than ever to whip up a sturdy little piece of bacon in minutes! Just don't eat it, OK?

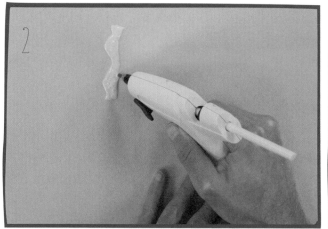

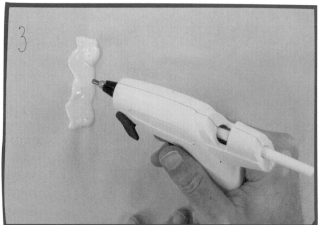

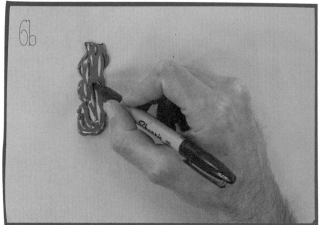

1. On your heat-resistant work surface, set up a ruler to use as your guide.

2. Draw a squiggly 3" (7.5cm) line of Mod Melt and follow that line back down, slightly overlapping it.

3. Overlap another line going up, making sure that it's squiggly like bacon.

4. Wait for it to cool (about 5 minutes).

5. Draw red lines up and down the bacon, leaving bits of white (the fat) to peek through.

6. Add brown streaks with a regular Sharpie.

7. Follow steps 5 and 6 to decorate both sides.

8. Drill a hole toward the top, add a jump ring and secure it onto the keychain with pliers.

Glitter and Gear Mosaics

Her Glittered Faux Broken Glass Mirror

Mirror, mirror, on the wall, who is the glitteriest one of all? You are, if you make one if these faux mosaic mirrors! I'm smitten over this technique, which saves time and money and can be hung off of a few thumbtacks!

TOOLS AND MATERIALS

9" (23cm) round papier-mâché lid

4" (10cm) round mirror

Spackling paste

Paste spreader

Fine-grit sandpaper

Quick-dry super glue

Craft knife

Pencil or ballpoint pen

Parchment paper

Permanent marker

Disposable gloves

Clear acetate or binder cover plastic

Mod Podge

Glitter in your choice of colors

Foam brush

Decorative paper (optional)

1. Apply a thin layer of Mod Podge to the acetate and add glitter. Have fun and do multiple sheets!

2. While you wait for the Mod Podge to dry, trace your mirror onto the papier-mâché lid using a pencil or ballpoint pen.

3. With the craft knife, carefully cut out the circle ⅓" (8mm) inside of the line you traced.

4. Trace the lid onto the parchment paper using the permanent marker. Be sure not to touch the lid with the marker.

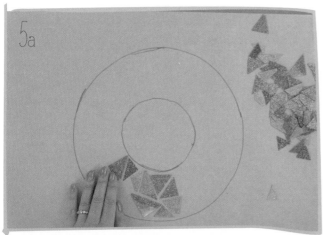

5. Once your glitter sheets are completely dry, cut out triangle tiles and arrange them onto the template, glittered side up, keeping the tiles ¼" (6mm) away from all the edges.

6. Using a spreader or an old credit card, evenly spread the spackling paste ¼" (6mm) thick across the top of the lid.

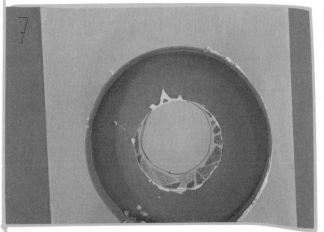

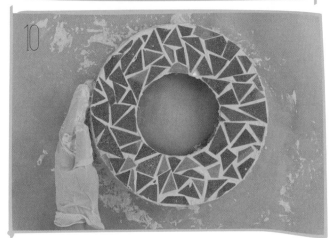

7. Flip the lid over and place it on top of your design.

8. Gently lift up the lid and look at your design.

9. Put on your gloves and gently push down onto each tile and nudge the edge pieces away from the edge. Don't worry about the paste bulging.

10. Add paste to the side of the project with gloved hands.

11. Let everything dry overnight.

12. Gently sand the bulges and rough spots out of the dried paste, making sure not to scuff the tiles. People with asthma issues may want to use a respirator.

13. Add a strip of super glue around the inside mirror hole and place the mirror on top.

14. If desired, cover the back of the mirror with a decorative piece of paper.

His Antiqued Agate Key Hanger

Acetate or clear plastic can be a whole lot of creative fun when you add various colors of alcohol ink. Dab, drop and smudge your way to the perfect faux antiqued agate tiles for your mosaic, then add some functionality to your art by adding key hooks to the bottom of your canvas.

TOOLS & MATERIALS

Small canvas

Spackling paste

Paste spreader

Fine-grit sandpaper

Parchment paper

Permanent marker

Disposable gloves

Clear acetate or binder cover plastic

Alcohol inks in various colors

Alcohol ink dauber or makeup sponge

Hooks to hang keys

Designer Tip

The color combinations and design ideas are endless with this quick technique. Just remember to keep this artwork out of bathrooms and areas that are exposed to moisture.

1. Using various alcohol ink colors, create a few sheets of marbled and textured acetate by dripping alcohol inks onto the sheets and daubing around as desired.

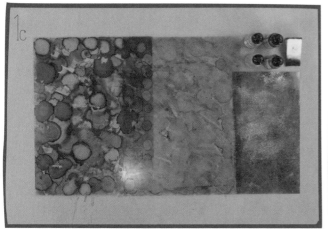

2. Trace the canvas shape onto the parchment paper with a permanent marker. Make sure you don't touch the canvas with the marker.

3. Cut out and arrange various shaped tiles onto the template, keeping the tiles ¼" (6mm) away from the edges.

4. Follow steps 6–12 for Her Glittered Faux Broken Glass Mirror.

5. Add hooks to the bottom of the canvas by first drilling small pilot holes and then screwing in the hooks.

Fabrication
Manipulating Fabric & More

Patchiliques

Zom-Bushk

DIY
OR DIE
TRYING

His Fake Stitch Zombie Patch

Patchliques are a great personalized creative project for parties. Either make some as favors for your guests to take home, or give guests the option to easily personalize their own patches with a few layers of fabric and a fabric marker for faux stitching. Design your own or flip to page 185 and use our craft- and zombie-themed designs.

TOOLS & MATERIALS

Double-sided interfacing such as Pellon's Wonder-Under

T-shirt transfer paper for dark fabric

Different colored fabric scraps

Inkjet printer

Fabric scissors

Fabric marker

Iron

Parchment paper

Your own designs or our designs from page 185

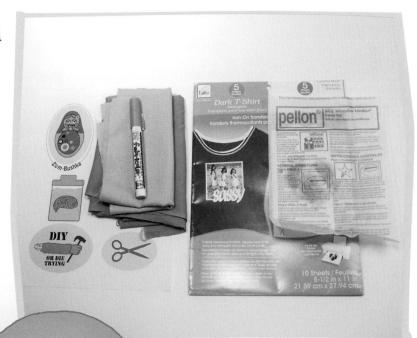

Designer Tip

Check out step 5 of Her Real Stitch Patchlique for instructions on adhering Patchliques to items

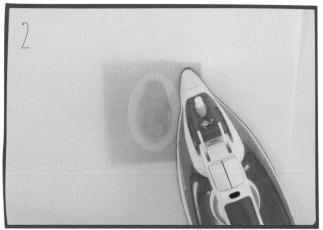

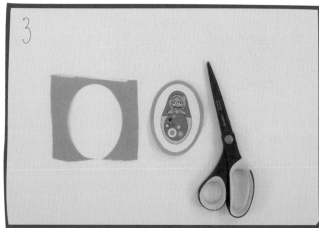

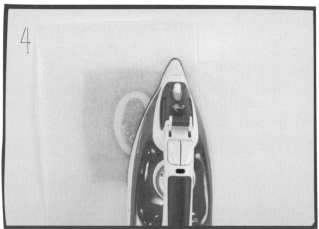

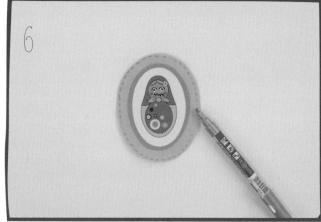

1. Print your design onto dark T-shirt transfer paper, cut out and peel off paper backing (if necessary).

2. Make a sandwich with the design on top (usually face up) of a piece of fabric, and the fabric on top of the rough side of the interfacing. Place parchment paper over the design and iron using the cotton/no steam setting. All pieces should fuse together.

3. Cut out the design, leaving a border of fabric.

4. Peel away the interfacing backing from the fabric and make another sandwich on top of a larger piece of fabric that has interfacing rough side up. Again, place the parchment paper over the design and iron on the cotton/no steam setting.

5. Cut away the excess fabric and leave another border.

6. Add faux stitching with a fabric marker.

Her Real Stitch Patchlique

Although I love Cliff's faux stitch Patchlique, I think this project offers a unique opportunity for beginners and seasoned creative types to enjoy the fun stitch patterns that often go unused on sewing machines.

TOOLS & MATERIALS

Double-sided interfacing such as Pellon's Wonder-Under

T-shirt transfer paper for dark fabric

Cotton fabric that coordinates with your design

Inkjet printer

Iron

Tack cloth, linen towel or parchment paper (for ironing)

Pinking shears

Sewing machine or needle and thread

Your own designs or our designs from page 185

Designer Tip

We use a wooden cutting board for our patchliques since most all transfer papers require a flat surface while ironing.

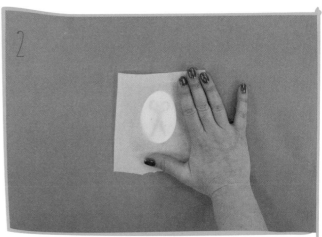

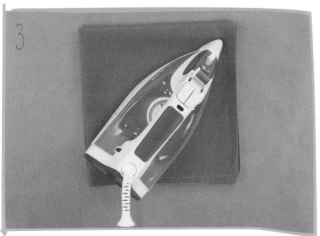

1. Print your design onto the transfer paper, then cut it out. Also cut a piece of fabric and a piece of interfacing a bit larger than your paper design.

2. Stack the fabric onto the rough side of the interfacing and place the transfer paper onto the fabric. Depending on the transfer paper, you may need to place it either design up or design down on the fabric.

3. Set your iron to a cotton heat setting with no steam. Iron everything together with a tack cloth or linen towel on top.

4. Use pinking shears to cut a decorative border around the edge.

5. Add a decorative border to your patch by using the fancy stitches on your sewing machine.

6. When you want to adhere your new Patchlique to an item, just use parchment paper to cover the entire item, a flat surface and a cotton setting with no steam on the iron.

Designer Tip

Our rule of thumb is to always use parchment paper between the project and the iron, but it's also nice to have parchment paper below the project in case of melt-over.

Felt Monogram Pillows

Her Girly Template Monogram Pillow

The possibilities are endless with these personalized felt monogram pillows. Get crazy crafty with random unmeasured angles (like Cliff did) or create a feminine floral pattern using an easy-to-create paper stencil.

TOOLS AND MATERIALS

Utility knife

16" (40.5cm) pillow form

Sewing pins

Sewing machine

17" × 17" (43cm × 43cm) felt fabric

17" × 17" (43cm × 43cm) cotton fabric in a color to contrast your felt

Two 17" × 11¹/₂" (43cm × 29cm) felt panels for the back

Scissors

Fabric pen

Iron

Printer

17"× 17" (43cm × 43cm) paper for template

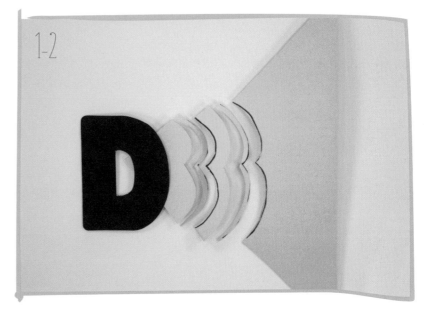

1-2

1. Print your monogram onto regular paper at Cooper 275pt font. Use a utility knife to cut it out.

2. Fold your 17" × 17" (43cm × 43cm) template paper two times. Starting in the center corner (like on a snowflake), cut a swoopy line of your choice. Make sure it's large enough to fit your monogram letter when it's unfolded.

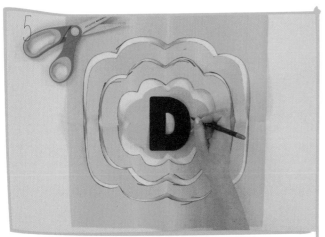

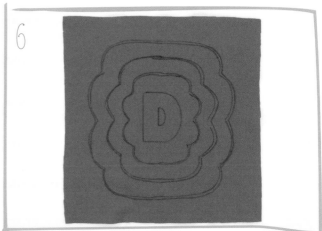

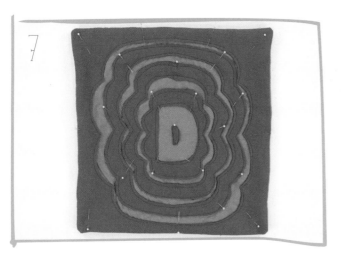

3. Keep cutting the same pattern every 1½"
(3.8cm). This should create three rings. Be sure
to allow 2" (5cm) between the last cut and the
edges.

4. Create spaces in your template by cutting ½"
(1.3cm) off the top of each piece.

Designer Tip

Use the same template for multiple
people by tracing the monogram directly
onto the fabric instead of onto the paper
template. Don't be afraid to go crazy
with placement and ring size. Just
remember, the more angles and rings
you add, the more sewing you have to
do!

5. Unfold the middle piece and cut the monogram out of the center piece.

6. Trace the template onto the felt.

7. Cut out the design. Pin the felt onto the cotton.

8. Sew all edges with a $\frac{1}{4}$" (6mm) seam allowance.

9. Place main pillow piece and the two back panels right sides together and sew around the entire pillow with a $\frac{1}{4}$" (6mm) seam allowance.

10. Turn right side out and topstitch $\frac{1}{4}$" (6mm) around the pillow.

11. Stuff with a pillow form.

10

His No-Fuss Comic Book-Inspired Pillow

This project is great for beginner sewers like me because it doesn't require a pattern to look great! Every pillow you create with this technique will be a one of a kind. Proof is in the pillow!

TOOLS & MATERIALS

Two 17" × 11¹/₂" (43cm × 29cm) gray felt panels for the back

17" × 17" (43cm × 43cm) grey felt panel for the front

17" × 17" (43cm × 43cm) white felt panel for the front

Utility knife

16" (40.5cm) pillow form

Sewing pins

Sewing machine

Scissors

Fabric pen

Iron

Printer

17"× 17" (43cm × 43cm) paper for template

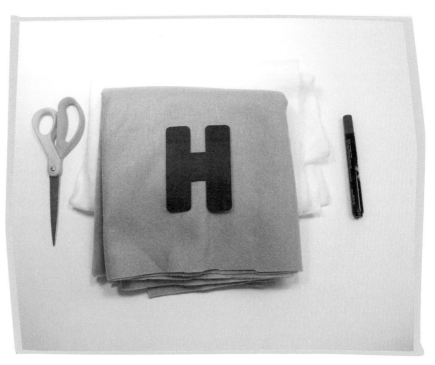

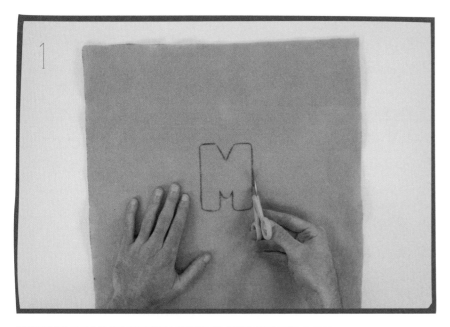

1. Trace a monogram in the center of the top piece of felt and cut it out (or use your template paper to create the monogram, then pin it to the felt and cut).

2. Fussy cut geometric shapes around your monogram every 2" (5cm) and leave 2" (5cm) of space around the edges.

3. Cut ½" (1.3cm) around the top of each piece.

4. Follow steps 7–11 of Her Girly Template Monogram Pillow.

Designer Tip
Still not a fan of all that sewing? Try using double-sided fusible interfacing to adhere your pieces to the pillow. Then you'll only have to sew the seams.

Plastic Pixel Bow Ties

His Geekish Green Pixel Bow Tie

With this handmade wearable, we took crafter canvas and some enamel paint and created a unique pixel bow tie that is not only eye catching but also stain resistant! Go be free and party like a well-dressed animal in this plastic pixel bow tie!

TOOLS & MATERIALS

Craft canvas sheet

Scissors

Ruler

Enamel paint or multisurface paint

 Paintbrush

 BBQ skewer

 Pipe cleaner

 Hot glue gun and hot glue

 Flat-backed pin

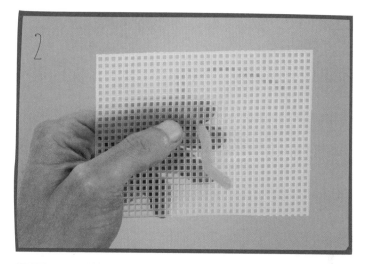

1. Cut out a 5" × 3³⁄₄" (12.5cm × 9.5cm) piece of craft canvas.

2. String pipe cleaner through the middle.

3. Pinch the center.

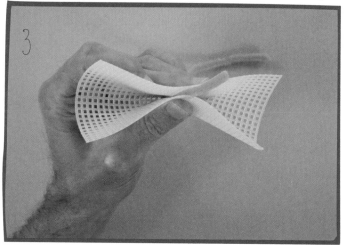

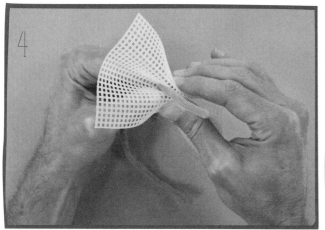

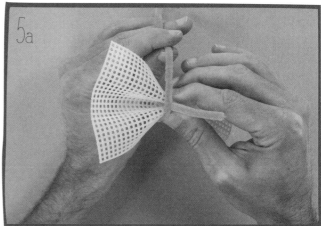

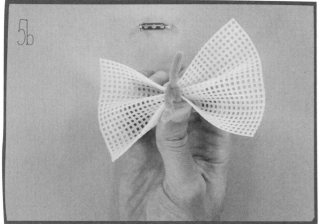

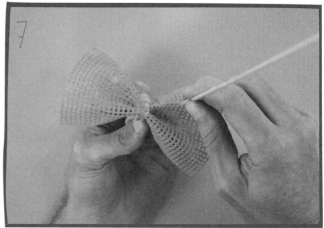

4. With your other hand, fold the outer edges down.

5. Wrap the pipe cleaner tightly around the bow tie and twist it closed on the back.

6. Paint the canvas with enamel paint and poke holes through the excess paint with a BBQ skewer.

7. Cut the off excess pipe cleaner and adhere the flat-backed pin with hot glue.

Her Metallic Fashion Statement Pixel Bow Tie

For a high fashion look, add metallic multisurface paint to your pixel bow tie and wear it around your neck, in your hair or even on your shoes! This is sure to be a crowd-pleaser among women and girls alike.

TOOLS & MATERIALS

Craft canvas

BBQ skewer

3¹/₂" (9cm) of ³/₄" (2cm) ribbon

Gold multisurface paint

18" or 24" (45.5cm or 61cm) necklace

Scissors

Ruler

Marker

Enamel paint or multisurface paint

Paintbrush

BBQ skewer

Pipe cleaner

Hot glue gun and hot glue

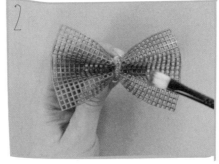

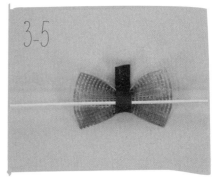

1. Cut out a 4¹/₂" × 2¹/₂" (11.5cm × 6.5cm) piece from the craft canvas, then follow steps 2-5 of His Geekish Green Pixel Bow Tie.

2. Paint with a metallic enamel paint. Poke holes through the excess paint with a BBQ skewer.

3. Create a space for your necklace by placing a BBQ skewer on the back of the bow tie.

4. Add a dab of glue to the top of the bow tie and press the ribbon into it.

5. Wrap the ribbon up and around the bow tie and skewer and secure it with glue.

6. Remove the skewer and run your necklace through!

Beautiful Blueprints

His Blueprint Glasses Case

Here's the perfect gift for those who like a soft place for their eyeglasses. Personalize it to your heart's content and use a glow paint pen to make the spectacles stand out in the dark!

TOOLS & MATERIALS

Thick, dark blue cotton or blue material of your choice

Fleece interfacing (as thick as you can find it)

Glow-in-the-dark fabric marker

Iron-on Velcro

White thread

Sewing machine

Letter stencil

Glasses stencil (found on page 186)

Ruler

Fabric scissors

Sewing pins

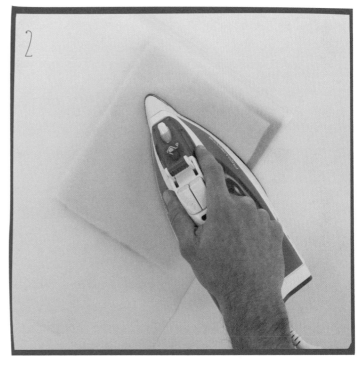

1. Cut a 5" × 10" (12.5cm × 25.5cm) piece of blue fabric and interfacing. (This size will hold a medium-sized pair of glasses.)

2. Iron the interfacing to the fabric.

3. Fold the fabric lengthwise and cut the corners off the top.

4. Fold the fabric at the 4" (10cm) mark and iron the fuzzy side of the Velcro to the center about a ½" (1.3cm) up on the blue side.

5. On the opposite side on the fleece, attach the scratchy side of the Velcro at the top center.

6. Now fold the bottom of the fabric up 4" (10cm) as if it were going to hold your glasses. Pin into place.

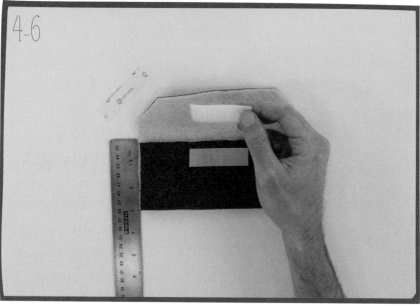

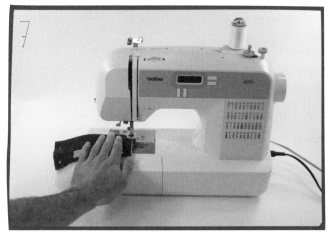

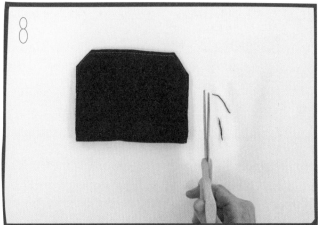

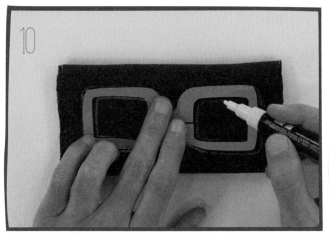

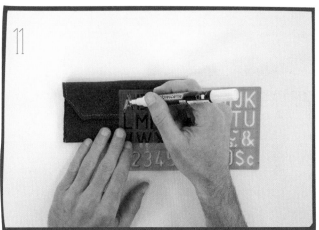

7. Open the top of the pouch and sew around the edges with a ¼" (6mm) seam allowance.

8. Trim off any excess or uneven edges.

9. Print and cut out the glasses template.

10. Gently draw around the glasses template with the glow-in-the-dark marker using light strokes. Place one hand on the template to hold it in place.

11. Wait until the paint is dry and add a design such as a stenciled letter to the opposite side.

12. Depending on the coverage, you may want to apply a second coat.

Her Blueprint Scarf

Make the perfect wearable gift by hiding secret messages, special dates, favorite objects or initials in this unisex blueprint scarf.

TOOLS & MATERIALS

1 yd. (1m) thick blue cotton fabric

Long piece of cardboard

Sewing pins

White thread

Sewing machine

Fabric scissors

White fabric pen

Initials printed out

Simple objects such as wrenches

Ruler

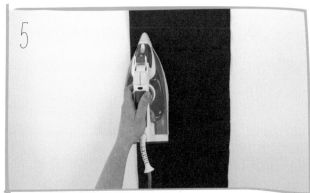

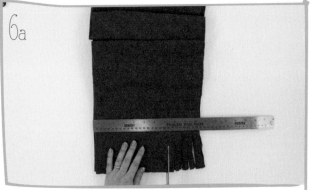

1. Cut your fabric and fold it lengthwise.

2. Pin along the open edges.

3. Leave 4" (10cm) on both top and bottom open.

4. Sew along the pinned edge, starting 4" (10cm) from the stop and stopping 4" (10cm) from the bottom.

5. Turn right side out and iron.

6. Cut fringe strips on the top and bottom about every ½" (1.3cm). Make the fringes about 4" (10cm) long. Don't forget to cut the folded edge strips so that they separate.

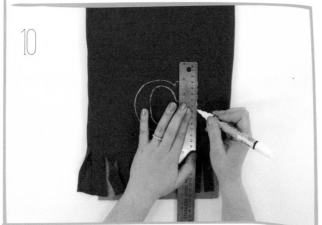

7. Insert the cardboard into one end of the scarf.

8. Cut out the monogram and pin it to the scarf.

9. Lightly trace around the monogram with the white fabric pen.

10. Use a ruler to draw angled lines and dashed lines.

11. Add little arrow ends to the solid lines and special dates or ages with inch or foot marks to disguise them as measurements within the blueprint. Also trace any other objects you would like on the scarf

12. Repeat on the opposite end of the scarf.

13. Topstitch around the entire scarf (minus the fringe area) in the longest stitch available. This will make it look like a blueprint dashed line.

Designer Tip

Drawing on fabric is not like drawing on paper. Treat fabric drawing as if you were using a paintbrush. If your fabric keeps catching or snagging just pull it taut and use lighter strokes.

Feeling Knotty

Her Knotty Photo Frame

If you are a fabric scrap hoarder (like me) or have an old sheet that needs a new life, then this project is for you! Grab your thrift store frames and get to wrapping!

TOOLS & MATERIALS

3 yds. (2.7m) of stretchy cotton fabric or old sheet

Large frame 16" × 20" (40.5cm × 5cm)

Small frame 8" × 10" (20cm × 25.5cm)

String or wire

Hot glue gun

Photo to display

1. Center the small frame inside of the large frame and secure to the large frame with wire on all four sides.

2. Cut 1"-wide (2.5cm-wide) strips about 18" (45.5cm) long from the fabric and tie the strips together. Wind the strips into a ball for easy wrapping in the next steps.

3. Tie one end of the garland to the larger frame and begin wrapping it around the frames.

4. Keep the knots from the inside of the smaller frame. (If one or two knots are on the inside, it's okay, but too many will block your photograph).

5. Tie off the fabric on the back of the larger frame.

6. Fill in any holes by stretching the outside pieces and gluing them into place on the frame. You shouldn't be able to see either frame.

7. Add knotted strips where appropriate to give your frame a more knotted appearance.

8. Use a dab of hot glue to place the photo behind the small frame.

9. Hang and enjoy!

His Rope-wrapped Lamp

The perfect little lamp for pirates and cowboys alike. Or just someone who wants a little lamp that appears to be defying gravity.

TOOLS & MATERIALS

8 ft. (2.4m) of 14-gauge wire

16 ft. (5m) of ¹/₂" (1.3cm) rope

Pliers

Wire cutters

Protective glasses

Candelabra kit

Hot glue gun and hot glue

Gold oil-based Sharpie marker

Electrical tape

Gloves if desired

1. Cut the wire to the entire length of the candelabra kit (including the electrical wire).

2. Fold the wire in half and twist, leaving a 2" (5cm) loop at one end.

3. Form a loose spiral shape with the looped end at the top (you should wear protective glasses while doing this).

4. Curl the loose ends with pliers.

5. Insert the candelabra fixture snuggly into the loop and wrap the cord around the wire with electrical tape.

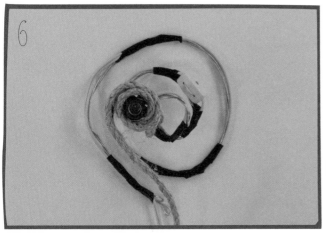

6. Start the rope at the top of the structure by hot gluing it around the light fixture wire loop.

7. Tightly wrap the rope around the wire and cord using hot glue and patience.

8. Once at the end, tie off the rope and secure it with a bit more hot glue.

9. Add a decorative spiral around the bulb by hooking an 8" (20cm) piece of wire to the bulb base and spiraling it up. Leave enough room to screw in the bulb.

10. Paint the switch and the spiral wire with a gold oil-based Sharpie marker.

11. Make sure the base of the loop is wide enough that the lamp won't fall over.

5 Feeling Festive

Personalized Gifts, Decor & More

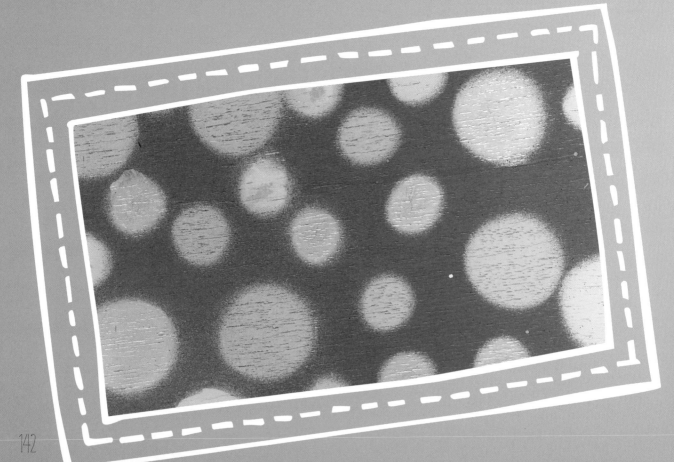

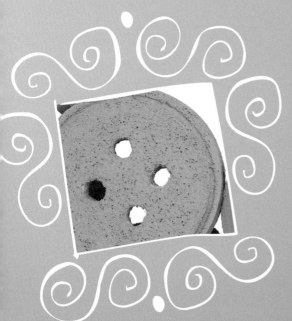

Foam
Garlands

His Giant Jewel Garland

Not only is this jewel garland perfect for video game-themed parties, but it's also great for pirate parties and diva parties. I can't believe I just said diva. . . .

TOOLS & MATERIALS

Five 5" (12.5cm) foam cubes

Five 3" (7.5cm) foam balls

Five 3" × 5" (7.5cm × 12.5cm) foam rectangles

Red, green, purple and blue acrylic paint

Fine red, chunky green, fine purple, chunky silver, chunky gold and fine blue glitter

Mod Podge

Brushes

Pack of BBQ skewers

8 ft. (2.4m) of strong string

Pipe cleaner

Foam cutting knife

Designer Tip

If you have an extra-large block of foam, the BBQ skewers will pull double duty and work as a painting and drying stick as well as way to create holes for hanging your garland.

Blue Jewel

1. Cut a cube lengthwise. Crunch each side of the four corners at a 45° angle. Carefully push a BBQ Skewer through. Paint the foam blue and add blue glitter around the edges before the paint dries.

Gold Jewel

2. Cut a cube lengthwise. Cut the four corners off and crunch the ridges. Carefully push a BBQ skewer through. Cover in Mod Podge and gold glitter.

Green Jewel

3. Cut the cube lengthwise. Cut off two corners and crunch the foam into a teardrop shape. Paint it green and add the green glitter before the paint dries.

Purple Jewel

4. Cut a cube diagonally. Crunch 45° angles into all corners and peaks. Carefully push a BBQ skewer through. Paint the foam purple and add purple glitter before the paint dries.

Red Jewel

5. Cut a cube lengthwise. Cut a small triangle off a corner. Cut a 45° angle off all the ridgelines. Carefully push a BBQ skewer through. Paint the foam red and add red glitter before the paint dries.

6. Add Mod Podge and silver glitter to the foam balls.

When everything dry, add the jewels to the string using the technique in step 5 of Her Giant Button Garland.

Her Giant Button Garland

Buttons are a colorful addition to any party, especially crafty parties, but these giant buttons would also make a great permanent installation within any creative space!

TOOLS & MATERIALS

Ten 5" (12.5cm) foam discs (not smooth foam)

4 acrylic paint colors of choice

Foam paintbrushes

2 rubber bands

BBQ skewers

Pipe cleaner

8 ft. (2.4m) of strong string

$^1/_2$" (1.3cm) wooden dowel

About a $4^3/_4$" (12cm) diameter glass or lid

About a $4^1/_2$" (11.5cm) diameter glass or lid

1. Make five buttons with two holes each. Press a strong $4^3/_4$" (12cm) diameter glass bowl or lid into the foam. Twist it around if the imprint isn't deep enough.

   Press a strong $4^1/_2$" (11.5cm) diameter glass bowl or lid into the foam. Twist it around if imprint isn't deep enough.

Intersect two rubber bands. Using the wooden dowel, create two holes an equal distance from the center.

Use this button as your template for the rest of the buttons.

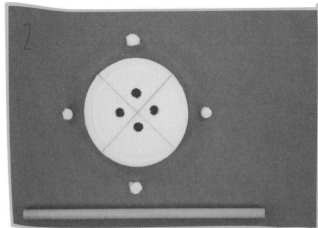

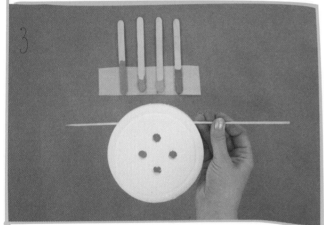

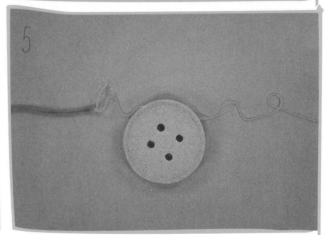

2. Make five buttons with four holes each. Press a strong 4³/₄" (12cm) diameter glass bowl or lid into the foam. Twist it around if the imprint isn't deep enough.

Intersect two rubber bands and, using wooden dowls, create four holes an equal distance from the center.

Use these buttons as your template for the rest of the buttons

3. Carefully stick a BBQ skewer through the upper quarter of the button.

4. Paint the desired colors on the front and back of the buttons and inside the holes.

5. Twist a pipe cleaner onto the end of your string and feed it through the BBQ skewer holes.

Personalized Party Hats

craft party!

Her Tie-Dye and Glitter Party Hat

Yep, I did it. I combined glitter and tie-dye into one birthday-tastic party hat using flat craft foam, acrylic paints and *glitter*! The best part is, you don't have to fuss with the mess of true tie-dye!

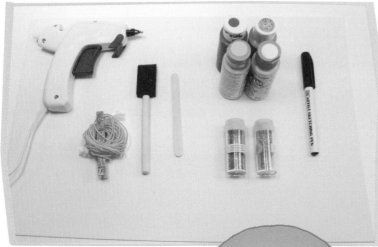

TOOLS & MATERIALS

5 bright colors of acrylic paint (I chose neon yellow, green, blue, neon pink and bright pink)

3 colors of transparent glitter (I used green, blue and light pink)

One 12" × 18" (30.5cm × 45.5cm) piece of flat white craft foam

5 foam brushes

Hot glue and hot glue gun

String

Marker

Scissors

Needle

12" (30.5cm) of stretchy string for chin strap

Popsicle stick

Foam letters or numbers

Designer Tip

Treat flat foam like canvas and go crazy with personalization, stencils, rhinestones and more!

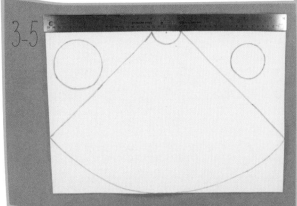

1. Make your hat template by marking your craft foam at 9" (23cm).

2. Tie a 14" (35.5cm) string to a marker (this allows 2" [5cm] for tying the string to the pen) and hold the loose end at your 9" (23cm) mark. Your marker should reach no more and no less than 12" (30.5cm) directly down.

3. Swoop the marker from side to side. This should create a rounded triangle.

4. Mark a 2" (5cm) half circle at your top 9" (23cm) mark.

5. Trace a 3½" (9cm) and a 3" (7.5cm) circle onto, the excess foam.

6. Cut everything out.

7. Paint your colors in a sideways smudging motion in 2" (5cm) increments.

8. Add the corresponding glitter color right after you have applied the paint. Tap off any excess and continue adding color then glitter.

9. Cut a jagged edge into the large circle and add color with the paint.

10. Cut the popsicle stick in half and glue it halfway up the larger circle. Glue the smaller circle to the back of the larger circle.

11. Glue foam letters or numbers to the larger circle.

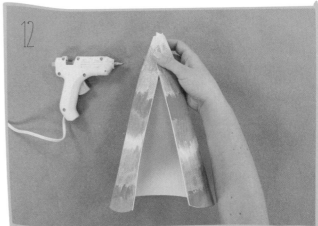

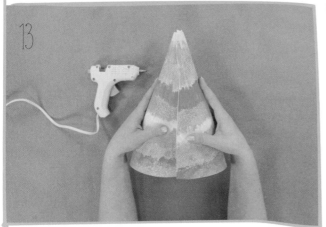

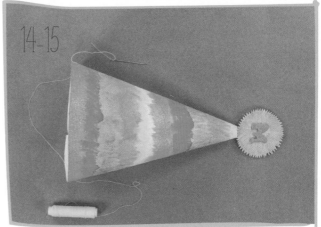

12. Form the hat by adding a 3" (7.5cm) glue line on the left side of the peak. Bring the peaks together and hold until the glue is dry.

13. Add a glue strip the rest of the way down the left side and bring the entire hat together.

14. Add hot glue to the bottom of the popsicle stick and push it into the top hole of the hat.

15. String your needle with 12" (30.5cm) of stretchy string and push through about 1" (2.5cm) from the outside to the inside. Do the same thing on the opposite side. Tie off on both sides.

His 32-Bit Party Hat

Add some 32-bit panache to your party with a fun, blocky green hat that screams, "I am geek, hear me code."

TOOLS & MATERIALS

One 12" × 18" (30.5cm × 45.5cm) piece of flat kelly green craft foam

Dark green and light green acrylic craft paint

1/2" (1.3cm) square wooden dowel

Painter's tape

Scissors

Needle

12" (30.5cm) of stretchy string for chin strap

Popsicle stick

Black foam letters or numbers (if you can't find black letters or numbers, buy some black paint as well)

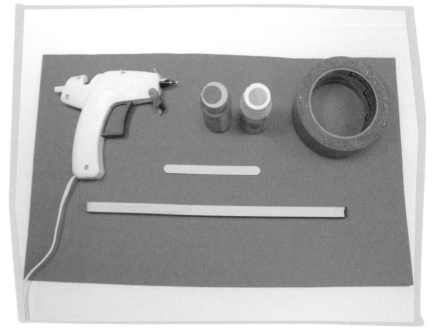

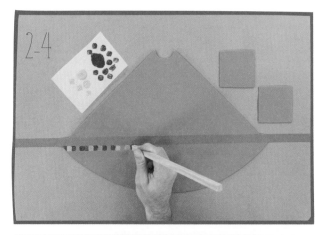

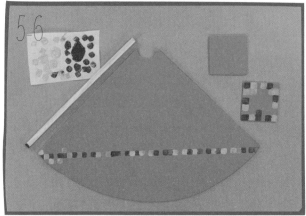

1. Follow steps 1–4 of Her Tie-Dye and Glitter Party Hat.

2. Cut two 3" × 3" (7.5cm × 7.5cm) squares from the excess foam

3. Cut out everything and run painter's tape from corner to corner across the rounded triangle.

4. Using both sides of your wooden dowel (one for light paint and one for dark paint), press squares of paint onto your foam, alternating the light green and dark green. Every so often, leave ½" (1.3cm) gaps to show the foam color. **Note**: Before you stamp the paint onto your foam, you must remove the extra paint from your dowel by dabbing it about three times on a piece of scratch paper.

5. After you have finished your first line, you can remove the painter's tape and work from your first straight line.

6. Don't forget to fill up the square topper with your pixels!

7. Follow steps 11–16 of Her Tie Dye and Glitter Party Hat.

You've Been Served

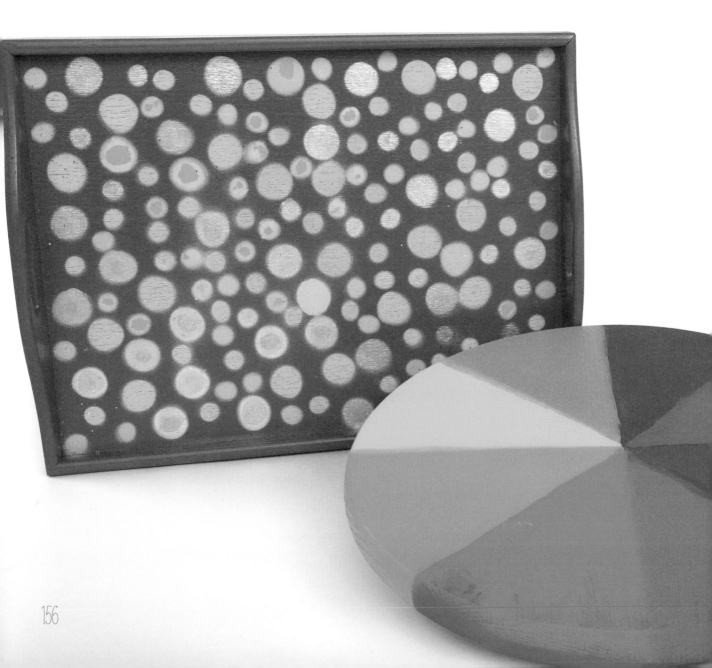

His Color Wash Lazy Susan

Spruce up your festivities with a kaleidoscope of colors that spin into a dizzying rainbow reminiscent of the Macintosh computer's "Spinning Wheel Of Death!" Deepen the colors by priming first or go with the washed beachwood look like I did!

TOOLS & MATERIALS

18" (45.5cm) round wooden table top

12" (30.5cm) lazy Susan hardware

Red, pink, orange, yellow, green, teal, blue and purple acrylic paint

4 long rubber bands

8 or more foam brushes (the more, the better)

Clear indoor/outdoor paint sealer

1¹/₂" (3.8cm) screws

Drill with a small drill bit

Fine-grit sandpaper

Wood filler

Optional: Primer (for a less washed look)

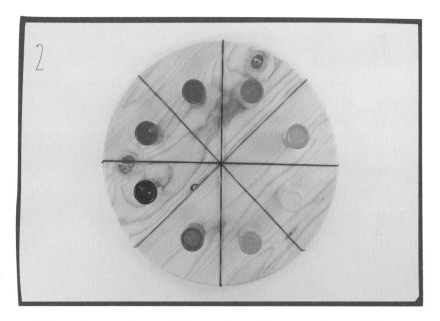

1. Fill any holes with wood filler and give the entire piece a light sanding. If you want to use primer on your project, add it after sanding and allow it to dry.

2. Create even pie slices by stretching the rubber bands around the entire piece.

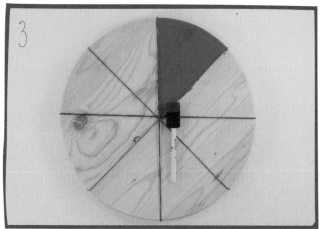

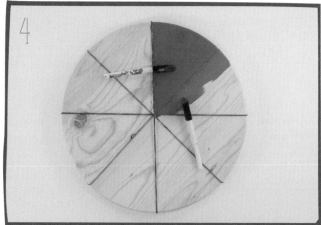

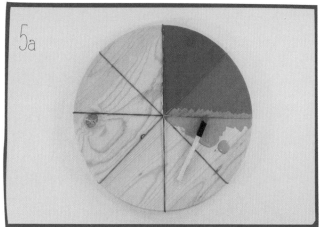

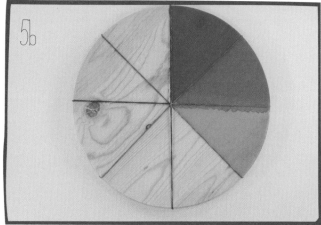

3. Add an even layer of red to a pie slice. Dab over both sides of the rubber band.

4. Add pink and use the red paintbrush to blend the pink and red together. Don't be shy about getting under the rubber bands.

5. Continue adding colors by overlapping the edges about a ½" (1.3cm) and blending with the previous color's paintbrush.

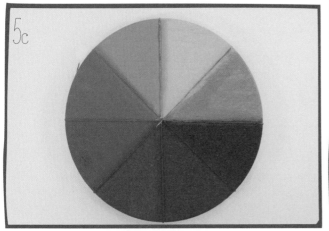

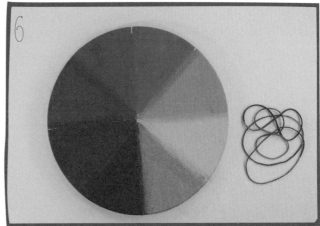

6. Wait until the paint is dry and then remove the rubber bands.

7. Add a second coat the same way you added the first.

8. Touch up if needed and spray an even coat of indoor/outdoor sealer on the top.

9. Center and attach the lazy Susan hardware to the bottom.

Her Bubbly Serving Tray

Use spray paint and glass pebbles to create fizzy little bubbles that serve up unique color halos on your designer serving tray.

TOOLS & MATERIALS

Wooden tray

Small and large glass pebbles

4 colors of spray paint

Fine-grit sandpaper

Plastic gloves

Tack cloth

Painter's tape (optional)

A well-ventilated space outdoors with a lot of newspaper to protect surfaces

Designer Tip

Follow the instructions on all paints and sealers because they have different drying times and working temperatures. Also, some paints require primers on wood projects, while others have the primer built in. With brush-on paint, it's best to use a primer when you aren't specifically looking for a washed look.

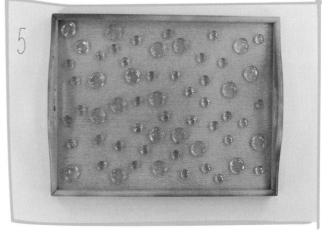

1. Clean the tray and give the entire surface a light sanding. Wipe away the grit with a tack cloth.

2. Lay the pebbles in the tray to ensure you have enough.

3. Remove the pebbles and choose your topcoat color. Apply it to the sides and handles. Don't worry if it gets onto the main part of the tray.

4. Apply the second color to the bottom of the tray by spraying directly down. It's okay if it gets on the inside walls, but avoid the outside walls by only spraying directly down.

5. Allow the color to dry and then add one-third of your pebbles to the tray.

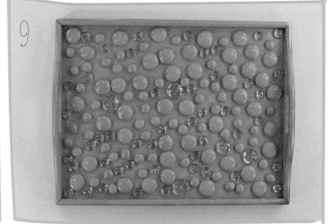

6. Spray your third color directly down onto the tray and pebbles.

7. Allow the color to dry completely and then add your next third of pebbles

8. Spray the fourth color directly on top of the tray and pebbles.

9. Allow the color to dry completely before adding the remaining pebbles.

Designer Tip
Be sure to remember that each layer of spray paint adds to the drying time of each following layer!

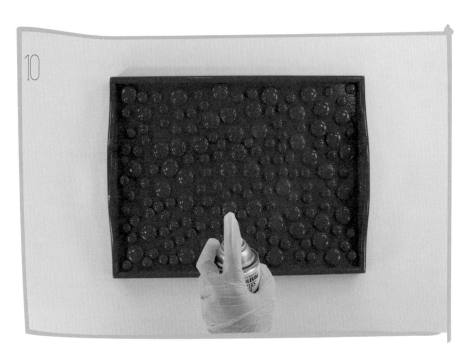

10. Add your first color to the top of the tray and all of the pebbles, making sure you fill in the areas of overspray from the other colors.

11. Once the project is completely dry, you can remove the pebbles and enjoy!

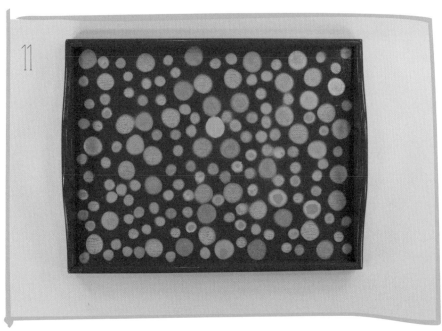

Booby-Trap Gifts

HAPPY BIRTHDAY

Wear the glasses.
Hold your breath.
Make a wish.

OPEN!

Her Glitter Explosion

Glitter seems to be a polarizing craft material. Either you love it or you hate it, which makes this glitter-blasting gift box the perfect gift for glitter-loving friends and glitter-hating foes! Warning! This booby trap is such a glitter-tastic blast that the recipient should wear glasses when opening!

TOOLS & MATERIALS

Gift tag that reads "Wear these. Hold your breath. Make a wish. Open!"

Memory keepers box or shoe box (Something that is already decorated on the outside will make your life easier!)

4 pieces of glitter scrapbook paper (Make sure it's thick like cardstock)

5 thick, wide straws (The kind used for milkshakes)

Glitter in various grits and colors.

Mod Podge

Hot glue gun and hot glue

Heat-resistant surface such as hot glue gun helpers

Scissors

File-sized rubber band (about 6" [15cm] long)

BBQ skewer

Bows and ribbons and/or other decorations

1" (2.5cm) glitter letters

Sponge brush

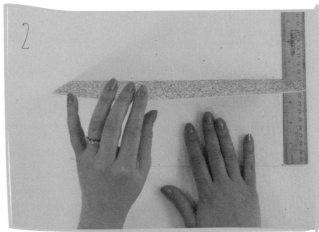

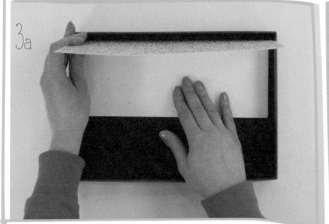

1. Cut the glitter scrapbook paper to size and adhere it to the interior of the box with Mod Podge.

2. Cut an 11" × 10" (28cm × 25.5cm) piece of glitter paper for the box lid interior and fold in half at the 10" (25.5cm) side (each folded side should be 5" [12.5cm] wide).

3. Adhere one flap of the folded paper to the lid and cover any open areas with more glitter paper.

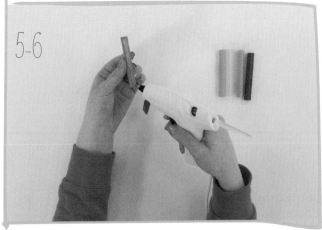

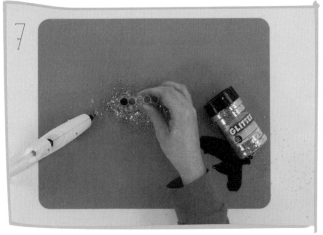

4. Spell "Happy Birthday" in glitter letters in the upper portion of the folded glitter paper flap. Use small dabs of hot glue on each letter to ensure maximum hold.

5. Cut five straws 4" (10cm) long.

6. Glue the straws together side-by-side.

7. Pool the glue into a line and sprinkle with glitter, then stick one of each straw into it. This will plug the bottom of the straws. Allow the glue to dry and cut off any excess glue with precision scissors.

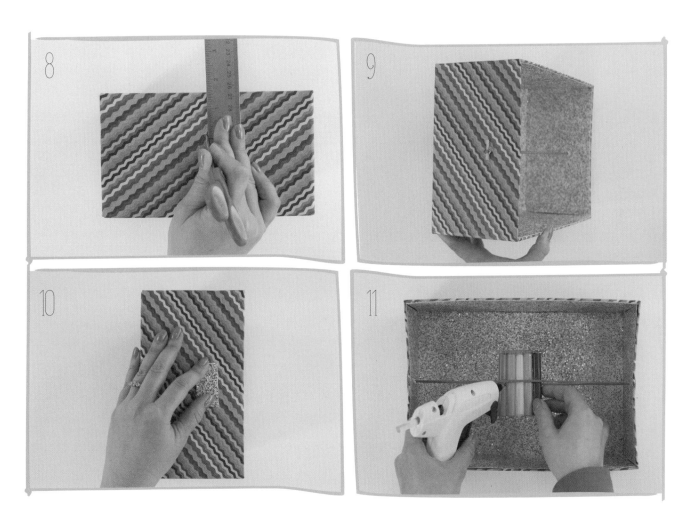

8. Bore a hole into each of the short sides of the box, about 2" (5cm) from the top. (Scissors work well for poking the holes.)

9. Run a rubber band through the holes and secure each end with a small piece of BBQ skewer.

10. Use a piece of leftover glitter paper to cover the BBQ skewers.

11. Insert the straws in between the middle of the rubber band and use a line of hot glue to hold them in place on the rubber band.

12. Position the lid against the box so the fold in the lid is resting inside the box.

13. Twist the straws toward you about 45 times. Let go to see how fast they spin, then twist them again.

14. While holding the straws, gently fill them with glitter. Don't worry about the excess.

15. Move the flap beneath the lid close to the straws so that the straws are resting on it.

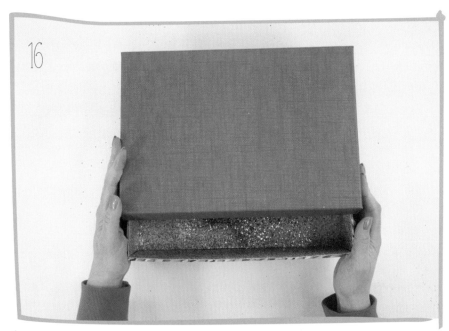

16. Carefully slide the lid onto the box without lifting the lid. You should hear the flap pushing along the bottom. **Note**: The flap should hold the straws securely in place, but we don't recommend sending this gift in the mail. The shaking may empty the glitter from the straws.

17. Decorate the box without turning upside down.

18. Add celebratory glasses and gift instructions!

19. Test the box a few times for fun and to ensure your tension on the rubber band is right. Sweep the excess glitter onto a piece of paper and pour it back into the straws!

His Faux Barbed Wire Gift

Give the gift of faux barbed wire, and the fun and games will last far beyond the party. Challenge everyone to pick up small objects at the bottom of the box without touching the barbed wire or ringing the bells!

TOOLS & MATERIALS

36 ft. (11m) black plastic friendship bracelet cord

10–15 bells (the more jingly the better!)

Plain, sturdy box (a shipping box is best)

Brown craft paper

Scissors

Duct tape

Double-sided tape

White Sharpie marker

Gift card or other gift

A buddy to help you twist!

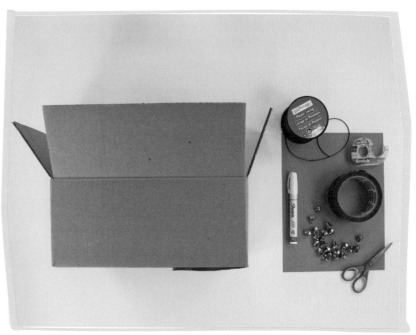

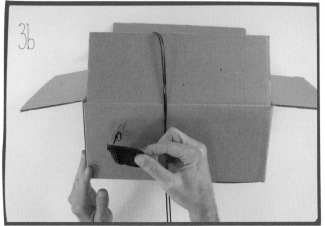

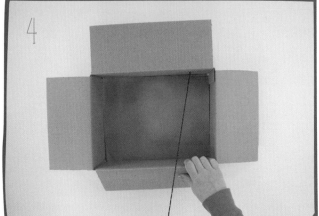

1. Cover the bottom interior of the box with a piece of brown paper.

2. Measure 36 ft. (11m) of cord, fold it in half and tie the open ends together.

3. With scissors, bore a hole through the side of the box and feed the folded end of the cord all the way through. Secure the knotted end with duct tape (this is temporary).

4. Have a friend hold onto the box while you twist the other end of the cord.

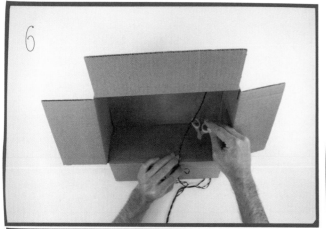

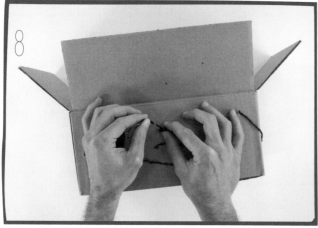

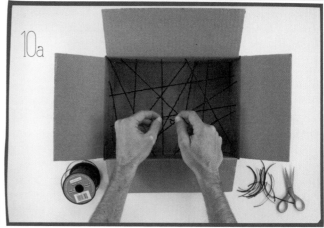

5. Once the cord is twisted like barbed wire, you'll begin to weave the cord through the box. Always keep your hands on the end of the cord to prevent it from unraveling.

6. With the scissors, bore another hole through the opposite side of the box and feed your cord all the way through. Secure the cord at the end with duct tape (this is temporary).

7. Continue to make holes and zigzag your cord throughout the box until the hand-sized gaps are filled.

8. Once all of the cord has been used, secure a tight knot at the end close to the box wall.

9. Carefully remove the duct tape you used in the beginning.

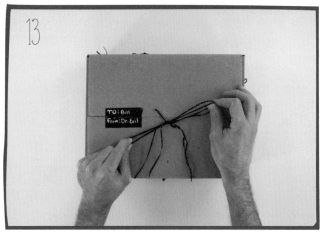

10. Cut 3" (7.5cm) pieces of cord and tie them onto the zigzagged cord. Cut off the excess. Now your cord look like barbed wire.

11. Tie bells to the cord with more 3" (7.5cm) strips. Cut off the excess.

12. Use double-sided tape to secure the gift card (or the gift you chose) to the bottom (this makes it harder to pick up!).

13. Top the box with more fake barbed wire and a strip of duct tape for the gift tag. Write the name on the gift tag tape with a white Sharpie.

Confetti Drinkware

Her Color-Blocked Confetti Wine Glasses

Add a personal touch to every special occasion with Sharpie oil paint pens!

TOOLS & MATERIALS

Sharpie oil paint markers in colors of choice

Wine glass or glass of choice

Stickers

¹/₄"-wide (6mm-wide) painter's tape

1"-wide (2.5cm-wide) painter's tape.

Rubbing alcohol

Scissors

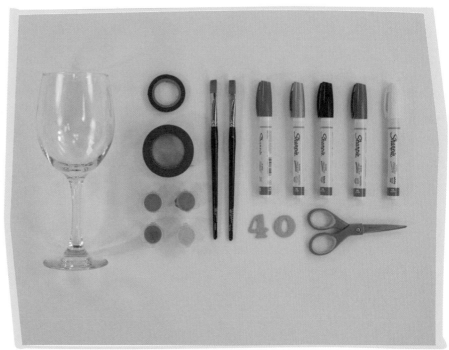

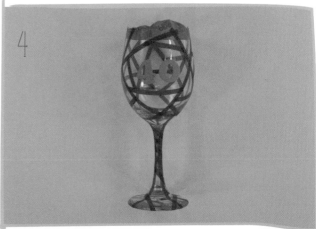

1. Clean the glass with rubbing alcohol.

2. Add 1"-wide (2.5cm-wide) painter' tape around the rim of the glass. This prevents lip contact with the paint.

3. Add stickers of choice (the number stickers shown were adhered to the interior of the glass).

4. Add lines with ¼"-wide (6mm-wide) painter's tape.

5. Fill in the open areas with alternating Sharpie marker colors. The numbers were traced and filled in, then removed from the interior. **Note:** Some colors may flow more easily than others. Just make sure you continue to prime them by pumping the tips on a scrap piece of paper.

6. Allow the marker to dry, then remove all tape.

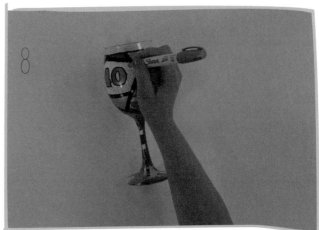

7. Fill in the taped areas (except the rim) with black paint or another dark color. This covers up any bleed or mistakes.

8. Add dots and lines to the blocks that didn't have great coverage. This works magically!

9. Once you are completely satisfied, pop the glass into the oven (while the oven is cool) and bake at 325ºF (160ºC) for 20 minutes. Let the glass cool down in the oven.

Designer Tip

These glasses should be top-rack dishwasher safe, but we always prefer to hand wash our handmade items, just in case!

His Champagne Confetti Popper

Everyone will forget about champagne when they see this confetti popper. It utilizes some simple materials for a fun, pop-tastic effect!

TOOLS & MATERIALS

Glass bottle with rubber stopper and wire latch

2 thick rubber bands

1 wide, strong drinking straw (the kind used for milkshakes)

Light confetti

Hot glue gun and hot glue

Pipe cleaner

Hot glue gun helper Poker tool

All of the materials from Her Color-Blocked Confetti Wine Glasses

Sharpie oil paint markers in colors of choice

Stickers

$1/4$"-wide (6mm-wide) painter's tape

1"-wide (2.5cm-wide) painter's tape

Rubbing alcohol

Scissors

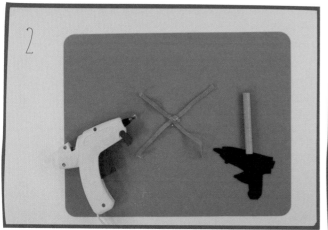

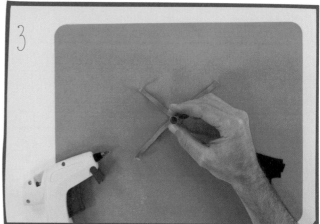

1. If you're planning to decorate the bottle according to Andrea's wine glasses tutorial, do that first. You don't want to bake this piece with the confetti launcher in it.

2. Cut each rubber band in half and lay one on top of the other to form an X.

3. Add a quarter-sized glob of hot glue to the center of the X and quickly stand the straw on top of it. Allow the glue to dry completely.

4. Feed the straw and the center of the X into the bottle, stopping halfway through. The rubber bands and the hot glue should make it a snug fit.

5. Add hot glue to the outside rim of the bottle and fold the rubber bands into it with the poker tool.

6. Push the straw into the hole about 4" and cut the straw to a length that will fit into the bottle while it is closed. Add more hot glue to the rim and wrap the pipe cleaner tightly around everything.

7. Your mechanism should be ready to fill! Give it a few pushes to ensure the rigidity and then fill it with confetti.

8. Push the straw down and place the lid on top.

9. Make sure the person who opens the bottle knows to open it like it's a bottle of champagne—pointed away from people and breakables.

Designer Tip

Keep the party popping by taping a few extra bags of confetti to the back of the bottle.

Templates

Templates for Miniature Taxidermy Bulletin Boards, p. 64

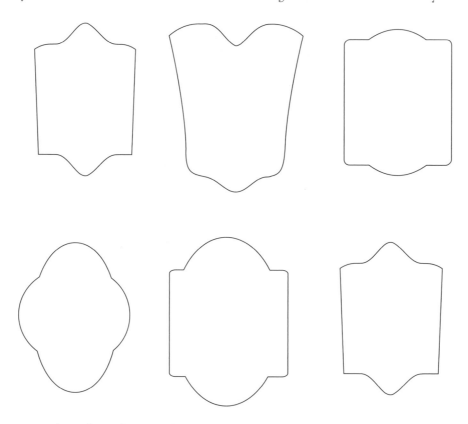

Templates have been reduced by 50%.

Enlarge by 200% before use.

Templates for Patchliques, p. 112

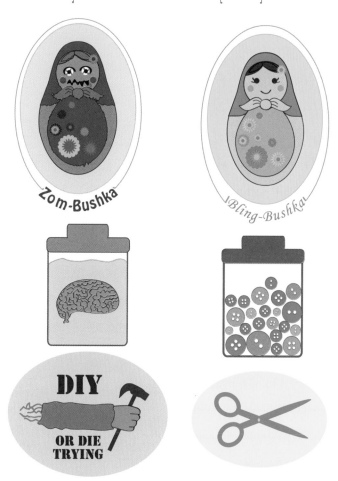

Zom-Bushka

Bling-Bushka

DIY OR DIE TRYING

Templates have been reduced by 50%.

Enlarge by 200% before use.

Tracing Template for His Blueprint Glasses Case, p. 128

Template shown at 100%.

About the Authors

Cliff and Andrea Currie are America's handmade sweet hearts as well as craft industry personalities, designers and inventors. Whether they are designing innovative new craft products or demonstrating brilliant projects and tutorials, they always bring an intoxicating mix of artful moxie and pure glee to their work.

Andrea, "Champion" on TLC's Craft Wars, and her husband Cliff got their start in the craft industry by producing the wildly entertaining Internet craft show *Craft-tastic LIVE*, which eventually transformed into HandMAKEMyDay.com, a popular creative blog where they chronicle their "he said, she said" adventures in crafting, cooking, home improvement and product development.

When the Crafty Curries aren't covered in glitter or sawdust, they're playing with their dog Gracie and enjoying an active lifestyle in sunny San Diego, California.

Index

Dedication

To those individuals and families affected by cancer, we hope the contents of this book give you enough sparkle to fight a good fight.

Acknowledgments

To Angie, Mike, Doris, Bill, Christa, Rich, Lisa, Wendy, Sue, Julie, Ramon and all of our family and friends who wholeheartedly support our creative dreams. To the craft community for opening your hearts and minds to us. To Andrea's wonderful doctors and nurses, who have gone far and beyond to ensure Andrea will live a long, glittery life.

www.fwmedia.com

17   16   14   14   13   5   4   3   2   1

DISTRIBUTED IN CANADA BY FRASER DIRECT
100 Armstrong Avenue
Georgetown, ON, Canada L7G 5S4
Tel: (905) 877-4411

DISTRIBUTED IN THE U.K. AND EUROPE BY F+W MEDIA INTERNATIONAL
Brunel House, Newton Abbot, Devon, TQ12 4PU, England
Tel: (+44) 1626 323200, Fax: (+44) 1626 323319
Email: postmaster@davidandcharles.co.uk

DISTRIBUTED IN AUSTRALIA BY CAPRICORN LINK
P.O. Box 704, S. Windsor NSW, 2756 Australia
Tel: (02) 4560-1600   Fax: (02) 4577-5288
email: books@capricornlink.com.au

SRN: U6489
ISBN: 978-1-4402-3807-9

Editor: Noel Rivera
Designer & Photographer: Corrie Schaffeld of 1326 Studios
Production Coordinator: Greg Nock

Metric Conversion Chart		
To convert	to	multiply by
Inches	Centimeters	2.54
Centimeters	Inches	0.4
Feet	Centimeters	30.5
Centimeters	Feet	0.03
Yards	Meters	0.9
Meters	Yards	1.1

Try these other fun titles!

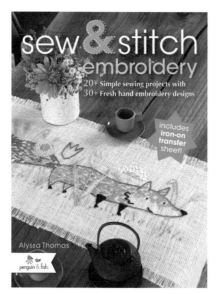

Learn fresh new ways to use your embroidery thread with these fantastic projects. *Sew & Stitch Embroidery* offers 20 fun projects with 20 variations and 30 new designs! Try both the traditional embroidery stitches as well as the new "big stitches" technique. This book showcases the flexibility of embroidery while providing endless inspiration.

Sew & Stitch Embroidery
by Alyssa Thomas
ISBN-13: 9781440232633

Stitch up these charming felt and fabric projects using step-by-step instructions and photography that makes creating them a breeze. *Happy Stitch* gives you 30 different projects, perfect for gift giving, home decoration and creative crafting. There's also an embroidery stitch library that puts all of the basic stitches for embellishing at your fingertips.

Happy Stitch
by Jodie Rackley
ISBN-13: 9781440318573

Join Miss *Emilly Ladybird* on a delicious Steampunk adventure in *Steampunk Tea Party*. Inside you'll find more than 30 stunning recipes for all types of cakes, cookies, jams and beverages, all guaranteed to delight your senses. You'll also learn simple tips and tricks that will help you create even more scrumptious choices.

Steampunk Tea Party
by Jema "Emilly Ladybird" Hewitt
ISBN-13: 9781440232954

Find more great craft tutorials at CraftDaily.com!